Disability in the Media

Lexington Studies in Health Communication

Series Editors: Leandra H. Hernández and Kari Nixon

National and international governments have recognized the importance of widespread, timely, and effective health communication, as research shows that accurate, patient-centered, and culturally competent health communication can improve patient and community health care outcomes. This interdisciplinary series examines the role of health communication in society and is receptive to manuscripts and edited volumes that use a variety of theoretical, methodological, interdisciplinary, and intersectional approaches. We invite contributions on a variety of health communication topics including but not limited to health communication in a digital age; race, gender, ethnicity, class, physical abilities, and health communication; critical approaches to health communication; feminisms and health communication; LGBTQIA health; interpersonal health communication perspectives; rhetorical approaches to health communication; organizational approaches to health communication; health campaigns, media effects, and health communication; multicultural approaches to health communication; and international health communication. This series is open to contributions from scholars representing communication, women's and gender studies, public health, health education, discursive analyses of medical rhetoric, and other disciplines whose work interrogates and explores these topics. Successful proposals will be accessible to an interdisciplinary audience, advance our understanding of contemporary approaches to health communication, and enrich our conversations about the importance of health communication in today's health landscape.

Recent Titles in This Series

Disability in the Media: Examining Stigma and Identity by Tracy R. Worrell
Reifying Women's Experiences with Invisible Illness: Illusions, Delusions, Reality edited by Kesha Morant Williams and Frances Selena Morant
Discoveries of Medically Themed Media: Pediatric Patients and Parents' Journeys of Sense-making by Heather A. Stilwell

Disability in the Media

Examining Stigma and Identity

Tracy R. Worrell

LEXINGTON BOOKS
Lanham • Boulder • New York • London

Published by Lexington Books
An imprint of The Rowman & Littlefield Publishing Group, Inc.
4501 Forbes Boulevard, Suite 200, Lanham, Maryland 20706
www.rowman.com

Unit A, Whitacre Mews, 26-34 Stannary Street, London SE11 4AB

British Library Cataloguing in Publication Information Available

Library of Congress Cataloging-in-Publication Data

Names: Worrell, Tracy R., 1974- author.
Title: Disability in the media : examining stigma and identity / Tracy R. Worrell.
Description: Lanham : Lexington Books, [2018] | Series: Lexington studies in health communication
  | Includes bibliographical references and index.
Identifiers: LCCN 2018003869 (print) | LCCN 2018002351 (ebook) | ISBN 9781498561556 (elec-
  tronic) | ISBN 9781498561549 (cloth : alk. paper) | ISBN 9781498561563 (pbk. : alk. paper)
Subjects: LCSH: People with disabilities in mass media. | Popular culture. | People with disabilities. |
  MESH: Disabled Persons | Mass Media | Social Perception | Social Stigma
Classification: LCC HV1568 (print) | LCC HV1568 .W677 2018 (ebook) | NLM HV 1568 | DDC
  791.45/6527--dc23
LC record available at https://lccn.loc.gov/2018003869

Printed in the United States of America

Contents

Acknowledgments

There are a number of people that helped me in the production of this book and I would like to thank them here. First and foremost, I must thank the reviewers and editors at Lexington Press, particularly Nicolette Amstutz. Valuable insights and comments helped to shape and form this text into more than what I could have imagined. Also, to all the scholars that find (and found) the importance in examining communication and health or disability, many cited within this text and those that simply provided inspiration, thank you. Particularly and personally the scholars Dr. Heather Zoller who started me down this path, Dr. Ron Tamborini who pushed me to always think "better," and the late Dr. Chuck Atkin, an unfailing model and mentor.

I have many people that have supported me through this process both professionally and personally. Of course, my colleagues at Rochester Institute of Technology not only for granting me professional leave to pursue this endeavor, but particularly Dr. Pat Scanlon and Dr. James Winebrake for their mentorship and support. Dr. Kelly Martin and Michael Sullivan for reading sections of the text and providing me with feedback and encouragement. My parents, Linda and Roger, for providing me the life tools necessary to follow my dreams. M. A. T. & S., they know why. And, finally my son Brody, always the light after a long day of research and writing.

Introduction

Father Marx said "God is in everyone." Floyd Feylinn Ferell replied "So is Tracy Lambert" (*Criminal Minds, Lucky,* 2007). Ferell, a serial killer on the television program *Criminal Minds*, mutilated and served up Tracy Lambert to her rescue searchers in a stew. A mentally ill young man that was released from an institution when he turned 18, Ferell went on a cannibalistic killing spree, eating his live victims piece by piece until they finally expired. Also on *Criminal Minds,* one meets Tobias Hankel, a former straight-A student that was abused to the point of having Dissociative Disorder with three personalities. One of these personalities was a serial killer bent on doing "God's work" murdering sinners. The "Night Ripper" (Daniel Stephen Varney), on the program *Law and Order: SVU*, had schizophrenia, murdering four victims in 48 hours. A religious, family man, Varney becomes schizophrenic due to untreated syphilis, and he begins his murderous rampage. But maybe you aren't like me, and the slightly spooky thrillers of primetime criminal dramas filled with serial killers don't appeal as much as some lighter programming.

Even the so-called "cool" portrayals of cognitive disability in sitcoms come with problems. Sheldon Cooper on *The Big Bang Theory* shows many signs of obsessive-compulsive disorder which makes him appear socially awkward with few friends or relationships. On the same show, Raj Koothrappali, has such strong social anxiety that he can't even speak in front of women. For those who prefer medical dramas, Dr. Gregory House from the television show *House* has both a physical disability after leg surgery as well as having depression. House is seen as angry, surly, and socially maladjusted but like Raj and Sheldon, he is also a brilliant man, which of course is made more dramatic by his disabilities.

What do you see with these portrayals? What do other viewers see with these portrayals? That cognitive disability makes one a murderer? That individuals with cognitive disabilities such as mental illness can't be liked or have friends? Or, is it enough that mental illness is becoming more prevalent in the media? Is raising awareness for a serious health issue more important than how it is portrayed? After all, negative representations in the media haven't been and aren't limited to physical or cognitive disabilities. One of the most commonly used models for examining representation in the media began with Cedric Clark in 1969.[1] Throughout history, if one follows Clark's four stages of minorities in the media, minority groups are traditionally not represented in the media (as mentioned in the first stage of *non-recognition*). The first "sightings" of minority groups on television begin in the second *ridicule* stage where individuals are seen as objects to be mocked within the media. The final two stages move individuals into *regulatory* roles such as those helping to maintain social order and finally individuals are in the *respect* stage where there are a diverse range of roles, both positive and negative, for individuals within that minority group.

Many minority groups, such as individuals with a disability, seem to fluctuate between the first and second stages where there may be irregular increases in individuals with disabilities in the media; however, these images aren't always positive representations. The aforementioned serial killers are not the only individuals with disabilities that have been seen negatively as criminals, "less than" people without disabilities, or overall failures. Previous research has found that these negative portrayals can increase the potential of stigmas, change attitudes toward disabilities, play a role in shaping identities, and these portrayals have the potential to impact how individuals in the "real world" with said disability are treated by others.

As a Health Communication scholar, when I first became interested in the examination of disability in the media, the works of Nancy Signorelli stood out. Signorelli has prolifically examined the representations of minorities in the media (2009a, 2009b, 2016), including race, age, gender, and disability. In her 1989 work, *The Stigma of Mental Illness on Television*,[2] she found that while there was a small percentage of major characters with the cognitive disability of mental illness (3%), the majority were seen as likely to commit violence (72% of individuals seen as mentally ill hurt or kill others, compared to 42% of others). Individuals with mental illness were also more likely to be seen as "bad" and "failures," compared to other characters. Additionally, 75% of the individuals portrayed with mental illness were victims of violence. For those individuals with mental illness that did have a job, 51% were portrayed as failures. Obviously, these portrayals would do very little to reduce real-world stigmas of individuals with cognitive disabilities such as mental illness. These 1989 findings drew me into looking further within the concept of the media's relationship to stigma. Further and more recent works such as from researchers Beth Haller and Lingling Zhang (2013) and their focus on the idea of stigma regarding media representation and how stigmatizing portrayals may even add to the "oppression of people with disabilities" continued to bring more of these important issues to light in the research world.

Aside from the stigmas associated with portrayals, researchers have examined how the representation of individuals with a disability in the media may impact the attitudes of their audience. Understandably, many of the negative portrayals have led to more negative views of disability and individuals with disabilities. However, even when effects research found that positive portrayals were related to positive attitudes (for example, Ferrara, Burns, and Mills (2015) found that viewing Paralympic games including individuals with cognitive disabilities did increase positive attitudes toward individuals with cognitive disabilities) respondents were still reporting low levels of comfort (Farnall and Smith 1999), with mental health services in residential neighborhoods that might endanger residents (Diefenbach and West 2007), and some children, even after viewing a positive portrayal, still didn't understand the disability (Diamond and Kensinger 2002). These studies also provide more questions to researchers. Why don't positive portrayals more often lead to positive attitudes like they frequently do for other subjects (Pearl, Puhl, and Brownell 2012), why would positive portrayals lead to negative attitudes?

Media portrayals and influences on attitude have been found to play a significant role in the identity of individuals with a disability as well as how those individuals perceive their treatment by others. Individuals develop identities within their social contexts. If the media is playing a role within this realm and representations are predominantly negative, there could be an impact on the quality of life of individuals with disabilities. There is potential for stereotypical representation in the media to reinforce negative attitudes toward individuals with disabilities leading to further stigmatization within society, which may give two avenues to how the media presentation of disability may impact individuals with disabilities—directly to one's personal sense of self/identity and indirectly through societal treatment.

There is some research investigating the treatment of individuals with disabilities based on media representation. I was fortunate to work with Heather Zoller (2006) on examining the portrayal of a chronic illness/disability, and we found that individuals with multiple sclerosis were concerned about the public perceptions of their illness based on portrayals on the television show *The West Wing*. Of particular concern was that the show has made "the experience of their disease more difficult by negatively influencing interpersonal interaction" (76). Further research has examined the effect of stigmatization such that media portrayals may play a role in the social construction of a disability, which could reinforce stereotypes and advance discrimination (Englandkennedy 2008).

Throughout the aforementioned research as well as others, expanded on in the following chapters, several definitions of disability have been used. For example, Gardner and Radel (1978) focused on physical impairments such as paraplegia, blindness, epilepsy, and physical deformation. Klobas (1988) expanded from physical portrayals such as blindness, wheelchair use, and deafness, to include developmental disabilities. Chen, Feng, and Leung (2014) base their interpretation on the United Nations' definition which refers to people having "long-term physical or sensory impairment and because of various barriers, they may not participate fully or effectively in society equally with others" (429). While this definition most closely aligns with what is used throughout this text, I chose to use the World Health Organization's (WHO) definition of disability.

The WHO states that the term disability is an umbrella term used to describe impairments, activity limitations, and participation restrictions. Disability refers to the negative aspects of the interaction between individuals with a health condition (such as developmental delays) and personal and environmental factors (such as negative attitudes and limited social supports) ("Disabilities" 2017). This definition characterizes a large group of individuals as having disabilities and the WHO estimates over 15% of the world adult population has "experienced significant functioning difficulties" (World Health Report 2017, 27).

One of the challenges of examining disability in the real world as well as the fictional world of television is not only the variety of types of disability but also the differences within each. Internal differences, medication alterations, age, care, and socio-economic factors are just a few things that may alter the impact of a disability on the life of an individual. This text, however, does its best to address these differences within each discussion and acknowledges that the previous and current research into any disability is limited by the experiences of those examined and may not be generalizable to an entire population.

It is not the intention of this text to argue over the definition of disability but to present as comprehensive a view as possible. This includes any and all health impairments that may be even loosely linked to the World Health Organization's definition. Long-term illnesses and impairments that may be aided by the use of medications are also included within this definition. The use of the WHO definition is important to reiterate. I chose this broad World Health Organization definition of disability versus constructing my own or one constructed by other disability or health communication scholars. As such this definition is potentially fraught with debate. However, I feel that the breadth of coverage within this text is important and that including as many minority groups under the WHO or UN umbrella definitions only enhances the research. The scholarly research regarding individuals with disabilities runs the gamut of examining different types of disabilities within texts to learn how those various portrayals may impact individuals with and without disabilities.

Aside from my own personal interest, research into the presentation and portrayal of disability has been found to be important on a number of levels. On an individual level, self-identity for those with a disability has been found to be affected by viewing media in which one cannot relate to a character with the same or similar disabilities (Kelly 2001), or the character is seen as a very negative portrayal of a disability. On a social/community level, portrayals may play a role in the social construction of that disability (Zoller and Worrell 2006) which has been found to lead to potentially furthering stigmatizations of individuals with disabilities. On all levels, research has ended with a call to media producers. This call asks those in the entertainment industry to not only think about how they are portraying disability within their program or movie but also to first hire actors that have the disability highlighted (Raynor and Howard 2008). Sure, one can digitally alter someone to seemingly have missing limbs ala Lieutenant Dan (*Forrest Gump*), but who knows better how to walk on those titanium prostheses than someone that does it in "real life." Secondly, studies have called on producers to double- and triple-check what they are asking disabled characters to do on camera (Zoller and Worrell 2006). Finally, studies call for the realization that the "supercrip"[3] may not always be the most positive portrayal of disability (Kama, 2004). So, what are these portrayals in the media and how have they been impacting individuals and society? This book takes a look at all of this as well as offering case studies examining the effect on individuals with disabilities.

This book is broken down into three sections to further explore disability within the media. The first section focuses on what the media has been and is showing regarding disability. Chapter 1 starts by examining the portrayal of disability within fictional media. A mixture of meta-analysis and primary research, including current examinations of representations, is presented spanning over 70 years of research. This historical review is important as one can see how the media presentation has changed (or not) over time. The second chapter transitions to more of a discussion, versus chronological review, regarding the popular press coverage of such portrayals in the media. Rather than focusing on how the press covers "real life" individuals with a disability, this examination looks at coverage of fictional characters with disabilities. For example, the *New York Times* highlighted that Blair Underwood's character of *Ironside* was "Disabled, but still dangerous: 'Ironside,' the Series Remake, Has Its Debut on NBC" which focuses on the character and portrayal of a fictional person in a wheelchair versus a "real-life" detective with a physical disability. The third chapter in this section puts together the representation in the media as well as the potential image echoes or reinforcement from the popular press. The journalists' coverage of fictional characters presents mere exposure (the more we are exposed to a stimulus the more likely we are to feel a positive affect toward that stimulus—or a potentially more negative affect) or strengthens potential direct effects based on theoretical foundations. This one-two punch examines how individuals are first being exposed to a particular portrayal and then are being told by the media whether this portrayal is accurate/inaccurate or positive/negative. The final chapter in this section takes a brief look at other sources for possible image echoes, new media including social media, and mobile technologies.

The second section of the book focuses on what the media may be "doing" to viewers—the potential effects of these portrayals. While much of the focus is on individuals that have disabilities, there is some discussion regarding how those without a particular disability may be influenced by the portrayals as far as attitude or behavior. Chapter 5 is an examination of the impact of portrayals of physical disabilities on viewers, including those individuals with physical disabilities. There is also a discussion of the impact of the media on identification and the social norms associated with the treatment of those with a disability. This is followed by chapter 6 which is a case study chapter with primary research conducted by the author with individuals that are deaf/hard of hearing and the perceived impact of media portrayals on said individuals. Chapter 7 examines the impact of portrayals of cognitive disabilities on those with cognitive disabilities. This chapter also includes the discussion of the impact of the media on the social construction of disability and the treatment of individuals with disabilities. Chapter 8 includes primary research conducted with individuals that have varying degrees of cognitive disabilities and the perceived impact of media portrayals on said individuals.

The final section of the book focuses on what can be done. This is not limited, however, to simply suggesting accurate and positive portrayals of disability to media producers. Suggestions of ways in which the above can be avoided/fixed/helped include calls to action regarding media producers, caregivers, policy makers, and viewers. This chapter contains information for each target as well as information that would work with larger audiences. Additionally, throughout the text several theories such as cultivation, social cognitive theory, theory of reasoned action, and others are utilized to provide foundational information regarding the importance of this examination as well as the possible effects of the portrayal of disability in the media. My hope is that this text may aid others in their understanding not only of the presentation of disability in the media but also how we are all affected.

NOTES

1. I worried a bit about some of my references throughout being dated, though like Clark's four stages many references are still foundations in communication research, so I would continually scour for new, more current research. The sad reality is that while many scholars may be researching in this area, publications are still limited, particularly when examining a specific disability or the impact on those with disabilities. I have done my best to reflect both foundational as well as current research throughout the text.

2. As will be discussed later in the text, mental illness is a cognitive disability and will be discussed as such.

3. The term "supercrip" is often seen when describing someone that is disabled and either overcomes their disability to achieve a monumental goal or they are able to complete ordinary tasks as an accomplishment (see Harris 2009 for more).

I

What Is the Media Showing?

There have been hundreds of studies analyzing the content of the media. From traditional content analyses and thematic analyses to overviews and meta-analyses, thousands of hours of television and movies have been viewed. Newspapers, magazines, and books have been coded and pored over by researchers for decades, all to try and understand what viewers are being exposed to within the media. Much of the driving force behind this has been concern—concern about how what we may be seeing may impact individuals and society overall. In fact, the concern about television viewing is so great that legislation was put into place to enforce ratings of sexually explicit and violent programming, as well as keeping those programs to hours when children are least likely to be watching television (see the Telecommunications Act 1996 and the Children's Television Act 1990).

So, what is the media showing? Well, research tells us that fictional television is filled mostly with healthy, white men who can be cured of almost any illness or problem in 42 minutes or less and that newspapers are filled with facts and always speak "for the people," whereas digital technology and social media may be offering different perspectives. What the next four chapters will focus on is what the media is and has been showing its audience specifically about disability.

Chapter One

The Representation of Disability in Fictional Media

In the late 2010s, the television landscape seemed to be more ability diverse than it had been in decades. Becky the young cheerleader with Down syndrome (*Glee*) kept returning to William McKinley High School. Another actor with Down syndrome, Luke Zimmerman, continued joining the shenanigans on *The Secret Life of an American Teenager*. Also on ABC Family, *Switched at Birth*, a program that follows two teen girls, one of which is deaf, and their lives with the "wrong" families received strong ratings for the network. New to the television landscape, we've seen the short-lived drama *Ironside*, the reboot that placed Blair Underwood, playing a police officer, in a wheelchair as a result of a shooting. Michael J. Fox returned to the air in a show centered around his Parkinson's disease. And, thanks to the numerous criminal procedurals (e.g. *NCIS*, *CSI*, *Law & Order*), dozens of characters with varying cognitive disabilities, particularly mental illnesses, were acting across television screens. Of course, if one utilized the World Health Organization's definition of disability as an "umbrella term, covering impairments, activity limitations, and participation restrictions," ("Disabilities" 2017) one might further this "disability count" to include any characters that have any impairment restricting them from being a "normal" member of society.

Researchers have been examining disability in the media for decades. Some early work (Head 1954) found the portrayal of disability to be both limited when it comes to representation and negative in portrayal. In the early 1950s these findings may not have been surprising as this was before many governmental policies and programs were enacted to support Americans with disabilities. Some would argue that disability rights did not see much growth or change until the Rehabilitation Act of 1973 (Welch 1994). It wasn't until the 1970s that concepts of program accessibility, mainstreaming and independent living began to grow and be a part of national policies (Welch 1994). As awareness and national attention regarding disability grew one would expect to see this reflected in the media landscape. However, even research in the early 1980s found low representation and mostly negative portrayals (Donaldson 1981).

Perhaps the most well-known governmental policy regarding the civil rights of individuals with disabilities (in the United States) was enacted in 1990, the Americans with Disabilities Act (ADA). With hundreds of newspaper articles, trade, magazine, and television news discussions of the ADA, the passing and subsequent amending of the act has been highly covered across the nation. Did fictional programs reflect the same growth in "coverage" with increased representation of disability? This chapter breaks down the representation of disability in fictional media from the 1950s until today. An examination of the trends found in previous research as well as a comprehensive look at current broadcast television tracks the fictional representation of individuals with disabilities. More than reviewing the previous literature, this historical examination shows us the growth or lack of growth within media representation of disability. One can also see how societal influences may have played a role at these times.

As mentioned in the introduction, this study uses the World Health Organization's definition of disability; however, not all scholarly research has taken such a broad examination of the media. Many scholars include both physical and mental impairments in the definition of disability, if not in their overall examination, such as Klobas (1988) defining disability in the media as portrayals of blindness, wheelchair use, deafness, amputees, developmental disabilities, and small stature. However, the aforementioned Gardner and Radel (1978) looked at only physical disabilities such as paraplegia, blindness, epilepsy and physical deformation. Definitions of cognitive disabilities have included everything from attention deficit disorder to schizophrenia (for an example see Diefenbach 1997). There has been some disparity, however, in how to identify cognitive disabilities such as mental illness within the media. Some reports (Signorelli 1989) have required some type of verbal confirmation of a diagnosis (e.g., "We're so sorry that Jim has schizophrenia") whereas others have also looked at character behavior (Diefenbach 1997). For example, if the aforementioned Jim talks back to the voices in his head telling him to kill he does not need to be verbally labeled as schizophrenic. Ellis and Kent (2017) use the more social model of disability which discusses the ultimate social construction of the term disability wherein it only applies when someone with an impairment does not have access (such as a lack of ramp for someone in a wheelchair or computer technology with no voice assistance for someone unable to see). Aside from varying in definition and how to analyze media texts, the findings of researchers have not seemed to alter much across time.

THE IMAGES OF DISABILITY IN FICTIONAL MEDIA

Before examining the trends across time periods, it is important to define the most common categories of portrayal across the past 70 years as they will be discussed throughout the text. Nelson (2000) points out six stereotypes within disability presentation; victim, hero, threat, unable to adjust, unable to be cared for, one who shouldn't have survived. Through examining previous work and combining a bit from Nelson it seems that the majority of characters with disability fall into one of four categories; the *victim*, the *hero*, the *villain* and the *fool*. The first category of *victim* refers specifically to victims of criminal or violent behavior (see Cumberbatch and Negrine 1992) and also that people with disabilities are victims in life; they are failures or their lives revolve around their disability and dependence on others (see Signorielli 1989). For example, *Law and Order* has frequently used guest actors portraying a character with a disability as the victim of a crime (see *Law and Order: SVU* episode "Disabled" or the *Law and Order* episode "Damaged"). John Locke, a character on the television show *Lost*, is first seen using a wheelchair. When his character is in the wheelchair he is often seen as weak or angry about his need to use the chair and how dependent he is on others. In contrast, once he is miraculously cured his character becomes strong and stoic with great abilities for hunting and tracking in the wild. While research suggests that people with cognitive (specifically intellectual) disabilities may be four to ten times more at risk to be a victim of a crime than those without disabilities (Sobsey 1994) and in 2013 accounted for 21% of all violent victimizations (Harrell 2015), there is little to suggest that outside of some caregiving for certain disabilities that individuals with disabilities are more likely to be victims in life or overall failures as images might portray. Nelson (2000) also points out that individuals with disabilities are often seen in the media as the "focus of telethons" or needing a lot of external help for survival.

Seemingly, portrayals of individuals with disabilities as the *hero* would be regarded as uniformly positive in nature. This supercrip portrayal of disability includes some of the most well-known characters with disabilities, such as Daredevil, the superhero that is blind, causing all of his other senses to become superhuman, or Professor X, a paraplegic with telepathic capabilities. Some studies did find the portrayal of the supercrip to be positive or potentially empowering (Zhang and Haller 2013) while others found it to be unrealistic and negative. For example, Kama (2004) notes the role of supercrip is often seen as positive, someone that can "accomplish mundane, taken-for-granted tasks as if they were great accomplishments" (450) or as someone that can perform extraordinary feats. But, this positive portrayal may do more to construct the idea that disability is something that needs to be overcome or that one can overcome disability with enough determination. It should be mentioned that Zhang and Haller (2013) did find that the image of the supercrip did increase some of their respondent's positive attitudes toward being disabled.

The opposite of the hero, the *villain*, (or as Nelson 2000 points out, someone "evil and threatening") is a common role for individuals with disabilities in the media. Characters with disabilities were seen as criminals, violent, cruel, dangerous individuals that should be marginalized by society (Signorielli 1989; Worrell 2012). The copious number of individuals with cognitive disabilities on crime dramas presented as the "bad guy" makes this common role prevalent. A childhood favorite, Captain Hook is the first villain with a disability that many come across, and one can likely name several other movie and television "bad guys" that are shown as having a disability. Some even hold up the legendary Darth Vader as a poster child for the villain with disabilities stereotype (Moe 2012). However, there has been no evidence to suggest that individuals with disabilities have *committed* any more crimes than the general population (Diefenbach 1997). While incarceration may be a different factor than crimes committed, self-reports by inmates indicate that the number of individuals actually incarcerated with a disability does exceed the general population with inmates in prison (32%) and jail (40%) reporting higher percentages of disability (Bronson and Berzofsky 2015).[1]

The final category of common images of individuals with disabilities is that of the *fool*. This representation is usually linked with intellectual disabilities and encompasses a social pathology model where individuals with disabilities are framed as disadvantaged (Cumberbatch and Negrine 1992), less than others (Foss 2014b), or in need of social or economic support. One can go back to the Shakespearean era for some of the first "fools" that were presented with cognitive disabilities or more recently, Lloyd Christmas and Harry Dunne (both developmentally disabled) are the epitome of fools in the movie *Dumb and Dumber*. Aside from the problematic stereotyped framing, Ross (1997) reported that many times characters with disabilities were seen as "disabled" first and "human" second, reducing the human-ness of said characters.

These presentations are not unique to one time frame within the media. The following chronological examination of disability in the media shows that the representation of disability in the media has ranged from .4% to 11% of characters and has maintained a relatively negative portrayal across time with an interspersing of positive and/or supercrip portrayals.

1950s and 1960s

While the signing of the Social Security Act in 1935 established permanent assistance to adults with disabilities in the United States, in the 1930s and

1940s it was still very common to institutionalize individuals for even mild cognitive disabilities. Post-World War II the United States saw a return of veterans with physical and cognitive disabilities that began to shift society's attitudes and behaviors towards individuals with disabilities (Gambone 2005). Beginning in the 1950s the United States started to see a few changes in the societal treatment of individuals. Federal court cases such as *Brown vs. Board of Education*[2] allowed that all children deserved an equal education that must be made available on equal terms. *Wolf vs. State Legislature* found that excluding children with cognitive disabilities from public schools was unconstitutional. Governmental policies such as "Aid to the Permanently and Totally Disabled" were added to programs, and laws began to shift to provide individuals with disabilities more rights and services than ever before. Social groups also began to put pressure on changing public perceptions of disabilities. For example, parents of youth diagnosed with cognitive disabilities founded the Association for Retarded Citizens (now more commonly known simply as the Arc) in the 1950s to help educate parents and society that individuals with cognitive disabilities can succeed in life (the Arc 2017). These programs did face challenges with the media representation of disability. Continuing into the 1960s several more organizations were founded to aid individuals with disabilities (such as the National Association for Down Syndrome) and government policies continued to be amended—for example, the Social Security amendments that lifted the age requirements for receiving disability benefits and the establishing of Medicare and Medicaid.[3]

The 1950s and 1960s literature brought us many timeless characters with cognitive disabilities such as Tolkien's Sméagol (Gollum) and his arguable dissociative disorder or the psychiatric hospital setting of *One Flew Over the Cuckoo's Nest*, with a large cast of cognitively disabled characters. A few films of the era highlighted cognitive disabilities such as schizophrenia (*Through a Glass Darkly*), or obsessive-compulsive disorder (*David and Lisa*), or contained characters with physical disabilities such as 1953's film *Lili*. However, few if any television programs contained characters, major or minor, that had a disability of any kind.

While the 1950s may have started with a small percentage of homes even having televisions (.4% in 1948), by the end of the decade, 1958, 83.2% of homes had a screen (Baughman 2017). This increase translates into a television viewing audience growth in the high millions. By the end of the 1960s, with three strong networks airing full daily television programs and over 90% of homes having a television, there was expansive exposure to television content. At this time, researchers began to focus on the small screen rather than on just the content and impact of large commercial movies.

In one of the earliest examinations of the representation of disability and illness in the media, researcher Sydney Head (1954) examined over 1,700 characters in the media. He found that less than 1% of characters of the time period suffered from any illness or disability. One character was found to have a physical illness and 12 others portrayed serious cognitive disabilities, specifically mental illness. Head concluded that crucial events in life (i.e., birth, death, illness) are almost completely ignored within the sample. Further, Taylor (1957) found that, while limited, the television portrayal of the cognitive disability of mental illness was that the "mentally abnormal do look and act in ways that differ from normal" (200). This is followed by mental illness being a product of stress or misfortunes and having serious consequences for the "victims" as well as their families. Individuals with mental illness were also seen as "unfavorable" individuals compared to others within programs. While research is limited in this time frame, these two studies show that even in a time frame where societal shifts regarding the treatment of individuals with disabilities were becoming more inclusive, the media landscape was still limited and negatively portrayed disability.

Interestingly, Gerbner (1959) examines the use of censorship in regard to cognitive disability on television in the 1950s. His study, "Mental Illness on Television: A Study of Censorship," looks at the role that censors played in the airing of television content containing cognitive disabilities such as mental illness, finding that network codes at the time "caution against the exploitation of mental (or physical) affliction for shock or comic effects" (294). Censors frequently cut out TV movies with cognitive health content deemed inappropriate (using words such as crazy, idiot, moron, etc.). This may shed some light on the low percentage of individuals with a disability portrayed in the 1950s. As one of Gerbner's censors points out, if a producer spends thousands of dollars producing a program that is then cut by censors due to the portrayal of disability, "next time around, he will make darn sure his film is going to be acceptable before he starts producing it" (302) and the producer would likely do so by cutting out any mentions of disability.

There was, much like the 1950s, limited research conducted in the 1960s to examine the portrayal of disability within the media. A large focus of any disability research was related to insurance, government policies, and rights, and very little research conducted in this decade was concerned about television or media and disability. Although two articles of the time stand out, a 1969 article in *Occupational Health Nursing*, on the role that nurses should play in reducing disabling injuries and accidents signals to nurses that "we give them the old health routine about drinking plenty of water and getting plenty of rest; however, they already know this from watching television commercials" (Attenhofer 1969, 20), suggesting that even medical professionals at the time were in tune with the influence of television on health perceptions and behaviors. Secondly, Judy Codd (1966) had an interesting examination of "The Effects of Television on Mentally Handicapped Children" and found that television did appear to have an impact on children with disabilities in helping to learn information and "extend a limited world" but her examination looked at the broad spectrum of television versus the portrayal of individuals with disabilities.

Fortunately, later studies looked back to these decades, and they found similar results as the research of the time. According to Byrd, Elliott, McDaniel, and Rhoden (1980) in 1968, 149 television programs depicted some type of disability. The most frequently portrayed physical disability was paraplegia (from the original version of *Ironside*) followed by cognitive disability, drug addiction and emotional disability. The high rate of drug addiction and emotional disability portrayals are said to reflect the stress of the times, a reflection of society's concerns regarding the consequences of the environment. Byrd and associates found that the characters with the cognitive disability of mental illness were frequently on crime dramas as "psychotic killers" and rapists. Further, Elliott and Byrd (1983) mention failed attempts made in the 1960s to promote positive impressions of individuals with disabilities through films, but televising positive portrayals did not alter attitudes of individuals toward those with disabilities.

Overall, this time period had very little examination of characters with disabilities within the media. While some popular reports have gone back to track movies, books, and television programs of this time period, scholarly examination is limited. Of course, this is likely due to not only the lack of characters with disabilities on television programs but also the censorship at the time, lack of understanding of disabilities, and the limited programming options available with three networks. With the rise in programming options, there is a rise of television shows and characters when one moves into the 1970s and 1980s.

1970s and 1980s

Governmental policies and programs continued to grow in the 1970s and 1980s. The Rehabilitation Act of 1973 was designed to protect individuals with disabilities from discrimination, provide services for individuals with physical and cognitive disabilities, and provide equal access to all federally funded programs ("Rehabilitation Act of 1973" 2017). For those children with disabilities the Education for all Handicapped Children Act of 1975 required public schools to provide free, public education in the least restrictive environment for their needs. Laws and society were changing as well. Interestingly, the last "Ugly Law" which allowed police to arrest people for being disfigured or showing some type of disability was repealed in the mid-1970s (Greiwe 2016). The National Organization on Disability was founded in 1982 to promote "the full participation and contributions of America's 57 million people with disabilities in all aspects of life" (National Organization on Disability 2017). In 1980, the Media Access Office (MAO) was founded in Los Angeles to help producers provide more realistic and responsible representations of people with disabilities. The MAO encourages producers to hire people with disabilities to play the role of a character with disabilities. The hope was that this would create the most realistic representation of disability in the media. For all of the potential positive increases in the lives of individuals with a disability in the "real world," as well as encouraging media producers to hire actors for roles incorporating disability, there was not a large shift in the media landscape from earlier decades.

With the end of the Vietnam war in 1975 media producers began, in the late 1970s, to show returning veterans in film and on television. *The Deer Hunter*, in 1978, portrayed returning veterans that were both physically and cognitively disabled post-war. *Coming Home*, also in 1978, features a veteran in a wheelchair as well as an officer with PTSD. On television, *Sesame Street* first introduced characters with disabilities including a character that is paraplegic, a Muppet that is blind, and in the late 1970s actress Linda Bove who is deaf and played the character of Linda the Librarian for over 20 years. Mary Ingalls loses her vision on *Little House on the Prairie*, and Lt. Commander La Forge of *Star Trek: The Next Generation* is also visually impaired.

The seeming increase in characters within popular television programs that had a disability did not translate into an increase in percentages across the television landscape. For example, Signorielli (1989) found that 3% of major adult characters between the years of 1969 and 1985 were identified as having the cognitive disability of mental illness. Byrd, Elliott, McDaniel, and Rhoden (1980) found that 256 programs depicted some type of disability which is an increase from their 1968 findings, but they note that this may be due to the increase in PBS programming (totals from either year were not reported to gauge any percentage increase). Smith, Trivax, Zuehlke, Lowinger, and Nghiem (1972) found that 7.2% of programming content examined contained health-related information and that 70% of this information was inaccurate, misleading or both.

The 1970s and 1980s did see a significant increase in scholarly research examining the representation of disability in the media. Findings as to the percentage of characters with a disability shown varied across the board. Donaldson (1981) reported .4% of characters with a disability. Cumberbatch and Negrine (1992) in their book *Images of Disability on Television*, examine British television from 1988. Their findings report that 1.4% of all characters had a disability. The 1982 Cultural Indicators Project found that 8% of major characters experienced physical illness (cognitive illness was not included) and Wahl and Roth (1982) did not include physical illness but found that 19% of shows contained minor reference to cognitive illness. These studies included a more diverse range of disabilities than previous studies examining cognitive disability and highlighted specific diagnoses such as schizophrenia, as well as physical disabilities such as a lack of locomotion and dexterity, and disfigurement (Cumberbatch and Negrine 1992).

Elliott and Byrd (1983) began their examination highlighting studies that have found inaccurate and misinformed depictions of disability. However, their own findings show an "accurate portrayal of disability despite a neutral context" (42). The authors also note the possibility of a trend to provide more realistic portrayals of disability. Other research during this time period, notably Signorielli (1989) and Cumberbatch and Negrine (1992), report the opposite, with the first finding the cognitively disabled portrayed to be predominantly violent or "bad" and the latter finding that the disabled were often seen as victims in disadvantaged positions. These representations are mostly inaccurate as there is no indication that the disabled were more likely to be violent or criminals than the non-disabled (Diefenbach 1997), although, according to Sobsey (1994), individuals with cognitive disabilities may in fact be more likely to be the victim of a crime than non-cognitively disabled persons.

George Gerbner (1980) examined the portrayal of disabilities within the very late 1960s (1967 or so) through the 1970s in his work focused on "Stigma: the social functions of the portrayals of mental illness in the mass media." He found that 2% of major characters were presented with the cognitive disability of mental illness. Of these characters, 73% were portrayed as violent. Similarly, for females alone, the mentally ill were about three times more likely than females without a disability to be violent. He found that the principal image of an individual with mental illness was one of unpredictability and touched with a sense of evil.

Heeter, Perlstadt, and Greenberg (1984) examined the 1979–1980 television season and found that there was an average of 3.3 health related scenes per television episode, but that the depictions in the media were not informative. Wahl and Roth (1982) looked into programming in 1981 and found that 9% of programs in their sample contained a character with the cognitive disability of mental illness. These characters were generally white males with an average age of 40 and tended to have no specified occupation. They found that people with disabilities were portrayed negatively and frequently stereotyped as individuals that were "aggressive, dangerous, and unpredictable." Further, individuals tended to be first and only identified by their disability. Characters had no family connections and had little to no real social identity. Lauri Klobas (1988), in her examination of a fifty-five-year time period, including the 1970s and some of the 1980s, conducted an examination of film and television programs that feature disabilities, looking at a large cross-section of media. She found that there was approximately one prime-time "affliction drama" each week. She also conducted a brief analysis of each character and the disability being presented as well as the language within scenes with characters with disabilities. The media at the time frequently presented an "us" versus "them" mentality and use of the terms "cripple" and "looney." Once again, as the decades move on, networks and opportunities for programming to be more inclusive increase.

1990s and 2000s

One of the most significant policies in the United States, the Americans with Disabilities Act, was signed into law in 1990. The law, seen as the "equal opportunity" law for people with disabilities, prohibits discrimination against people with disabilities and that individuals have the same rights and abilities to participate in "mainstream" America. The Act led to widespread changes in organizations across America and for businesses that did not comply, expensive lawsuits. As the ADA and repercussions for non-compliance began to become more widespread in the U.S., further organizations were started to continue fighting for rights of individuals with disabilities. The American Association of People with Disabilities was founded in 1995 with the mission to "to improve the lives of people with disabilities by acting as a convener, connector, and catalyst for change, increasing the political and economic power of people with disabilities" (AAPD 2017). These events coincide with a rise in celebrities discussing their own disabilities (Christopher Reeve who became paralyzed from a fall from a horse), contracting an illness protected under ADA (the 1991 positive HIV test for Magic Johnson), and the increase in actors with disabilities playing characters with disabilities.

In the television landscape, the 1990s and 2000s saw an increase in individuals with Down syndrome in real life as characters with Down syndrome on television (Corky on *Life Goes On* and Tom Bowman on *The Secret Life of an American Teenager*). However, other cognitive disabilities were still portrayed by actors without any disability (that we are aware of), for example, Tony Shaloub and his obsessive-compulsive disorder on *Monk*. With the first iteration of *Law & Order* beginning in 1990 and *CSI* in 2000 the number of characters with schizophrenia, multiple personalities, and other cognitive disabilities also dotted primetime. Physical disabilities were still frequently played by non-disabled actors such as Terry O'Quinn as John Locke in a wheelchair for much of the run of *Lost*. Jason Street, played by Scott Porter, paralyzed on the football field on *Friday Night Lights* spends the rest of the series in a wheelchair. And, of course, Dr. House was famous for his cane, limp, and pharmaceutical addiction on the television program *House*.

Research in this time frame did not, however, find significant growth in the numbers or types of portrayals on television. While Cumberbatch and Negrine (1992) found 1.4% of characters in 1988 had a disability, numbers for later years in the United States were found to be similar if not lower. Diefenbach and West (2007) found similar numbers—around 1.4% of characters[4] were identified as having a cognitive "disorder." Wahl, Hanrahan, Karl, Lasher, and Swaye (2007) found less than 3% of characters to have the cognitive disability of mental illness, whereas Bond (2008) reports 4.4% of characters had a physical disability on children's television. (Again, it is difficult to compare trends when studies focus on varying disabilities and varying audiences, but it is still obviously a very small percentage of characters on television with disabilities.) Later into the 2000s, one of my own studies (2012) found that from 2006–2011, 11% of characters on television displayed a physical or cognitive disability. Two things are important to note here: 1. This study was one of the first using a very broad definition of disability and encompasses all types (much like this text) and 2. The majority of these characters were guests appearing in only one or two episodes in a series run.

Also in line with previous research, the 1990s and 2000s frequently showed negative or stereotyped presentations of individuals with disabilities. While Bond (2008) found the portrayal on children's programs to be morally good and satisfied with life, and treated equally by characters without disabilities, this was seemingly an anomalous portrayal of physical disability. Worrell (2012) found that roughly half of the 11% of characters with a disability were portrayed as criminals. Almost all of the characters were negatively or neutrally portrayed—even the non-criminals were presented as being troubled, mean, suspects, and victims. Labels such as "crazy" or "psychotic" were commonly used. For some their story outcomes did seem more positive such as *Samantha Who*, lead character Samantha who has amnesia and learns a valuable life lesson at the end of nearly every episode.

Wahl and associates (2007) had similar findings of characters with disabilities being more cruel or aggressive than those characters seemingly without disabilities. Much like Wahl's 1982 study with Roth, characters with a disability were predominantly white males that were jobless and without apparent families. Two-thirds of these characters were labeled as aggressive (while showing no distress about their violence) and characters were likely to fit easily into the villain model of portrayal. Their findings also showed characters to be negatively treated by others (67%). There was a distinct portrayal of stigmatization (62%) and frequent use of negative language such as referring to individuals as "crackpots" or "nuts."

Diefenbach (1997) analyzed programming in the early 1990s, finding that 34% of characters with the cognitive disability of a mental illness were portrayed as murderers, rapists, robbers, or as committing assault. When further crimes were examined such as abuse, kidnapping or other violent crimes, that number rises to 44%. He found that for speaking characters, offender rates were ten times higher than the general population of characters. Like Wahl's earlier studies, Diefenbach also found that individuals with mental illness were predominantly male. For an in-depth examination of a specific disability of the time, Englandkennedy (2008) does a thorough analysis of the inaccuracies and stereotyping of Attention Deficit Disorder, finding negative cultural stereotypes and the media portrayal of "ADD as over diagnosed, overmedicated, and questioning its legitimacy as a category of disability" (102). As we move into a time period which frequently promotes inclusivity and growth as a society, we can look to see if that is reflected in the media landscape and representation of disability in the media as well.

2010s and Beyond

One of the most significant medical changes for all took place with the Patient Protection and Affordable Care Act becoming a law in 2010. For individuals with disabilities two important factors of the law are the inability for companies to drop coverage when an individual gets sick (as of 2012) and as of 2014, one cannot be denied coverage due to a pre-existing condition.[5] In 2011, new ADA rules began to come into effect expanding accessibility requirements which aid inclusivity. Several local and state policies were enacted closing inequality gaps that had existed. Closed captioning also got a boost with the 21st Century Communications and Video Accessibility Act of 2010 (FCC 2010) requiring captioning for full-length television programs when moving online. Netflix also began offering captioning for all programs and movies in 2014. While programs and policies are not yet perfect and are continuously being revised, the "real-life" state of protections of rights and benefits has come a long way in the past 70 years. This includes the ability for individuals to view television in a completely new form, through computers, through time-shifting and using mobile devices.[6]

Within the media landscape, one begins to see more characters with specific diagnoses such as Max on *Parenthood*, a child with Asperger syndrome, or the aforementioned Becky and Luke, teenagers with Down syndrome. While the obsessive-compulsive Monk may no longer headline a program, Daphne (Katie LeClerc) from *Switched at Birth* and J.J. DiMeo (Micah Fowler) from *Speechless* are stepping in to lead the way as main characters that are deaf and with cerebral palsy, respectively. However, finding characters with disabilities on mainstream television is still challenging and a low percentage of overall characters on television are individuals with disabilities.

Scholarly research is also seeing additions in studies focusing on specific disabilities. For example, Avery Holton's 2013 study "What's Wrong with Max? *Parenthood* and the Portrayal of Autism" focuses solely on one character's presentation of Asperger syndrome. Holton's findings underscore much of what was found more universally in previous research. The presentation here, while seemingly well-meaning (producer Jason Katims' son has Asperger syndrome) shows those with Asperger's as negatively "different," isolated, and that a diagnosis should provide family and friends with great anxiety and worry. Additionally, Katherine Foss has researched hearing loss and representations of deafness in the media. While she found few presentations of individuals with hearing loss in the media, when shown she found that most hearing loss was temporary on television and even those with "permanent hearing loss return to 'normal' after receiving their hearing aids" (2014a, 896). Also, in her 2014b study she found that deaf frequently equaled deficient, vulnerable and incapable in the media and cochlear implants were the "cure" needed.

While at the printing of this text there has not been a clear picture presented of the numbers of characters with disabilities on television today, some early examinations based on quantitative analysis such as my own in 2012, as well as primary research presented later in the text show the representation is still well under the U.S. Census percentages on individuals with disabilities (19%). That health information provided is still not entirely accurate: "cures" in 42 minutes or less is misleading, and the media continues to perpetuate negative stereotypes. And, this is just in fictional media. What happens when we add non-fiction or news media to the mix?

NOTES

1. The information on crimes committed by individuals seems mixed as there may be a disparity between crimes committed and those serving time. There are several opinion- and fact-based reports that the overrepresentation in prisons does not reflect the number of crimes committed but is more likely a sign of prejudice or unjust incarceration. Further, as the current inmate statistics were taken from self-report by inmates it may be taken with a grain of salt.

2. In *Hernandez vs. Texas*, the Supreme Court held that equal protection under the Fourteenth Amendment extends beyond a "two-class theory" of differences between black and white individuals, but includes protections for any individual who is a member of a group singled out for discriminatory treatment, regardless of national origin or descent.

3. It is of particular interest to the author that 1965 also found the formation of the National Technical Institute for the Deaf at the Rochester Institute of Technology.

4. The sample total within this study is not clear. It is reported that there were 2,027 non-mentally disordered speaking characters within the sample and a total of 29 characters identified as mentally disordered; however, if those characters were also speaking or included non-speaking is not entirely clear.

5. While the current administration is challenging this law, at the time of printing this Affordable Care Act is still in place.

6. While smaller screens have been found to lead to lower immersion scores by viewers (Rigby, Brumby, Cox, and Gould 2016) there is still debate within communication research regarding any differences in effects across platforms when viewing television content.

Chapter Two

A Popular Press Discussion of Portrayals in the Media

In June of 2016, CBS News reported that "*Finding Dory* shatters stereotypes about disabilities" (Ninan 2016). In essence, a fish has done what no other film or television program character could do—help others understand a cognitive disability such as mental illness. This type of reporting regarding disabilities in fictional media is not new. While a number of articles report on the fact that there are few roles for actors with disabilities or even characters with disabilities in the media, articles frequently highlight the accolades of a character with a disability on a program as the "first" or as a great example. For instance, Geri Jewell from *The Facts of Life* has been reported as the "first person to appear on network television with a visible disability" (*South Bend Tribune* 2004), which, of course, discounts actors playing characters with visible disabilities prior to 1980 (sorry, Lou Ferrigno of *The Incredible Hulk*). And, don't tell *Breaking Bad* star RJ Mitte that five years as Walter White Jr. on the critically acclaimed show was overlooked by the *New York Post* in their article, "'Speechless' star Micah Fowler's trailblazing role" (both gentleman have cerebral palsy) (Starr 2016). But, these types of descriptions fit well with headlines calling for more characters with disabilities in the media, such as *The National* headline that "the disabled acting community works to end of decades of 'invisibility'" (Kennedy 2012). After all, if earlier characters weren't noticed by the very people covering entertainment news, how could a more typical audience be expected to notice?

Once noticed, however, how are individuals with disabilities being discussed in the popular press? Researchers associated with the National Center on Disability and Journalism at Arizona State University created a *Disability Language Style Guide* (2017) to aid journalists and others on the "appropriate and accurate" language to be used when referring to individuals living with disability. While this text does not cover specific instances in which a fictional character is discussed differently than a nonfiction individual, the words, phrases and sensitivity should be the same. That is, a fictional character with a disability should be covered in the popular press using the same appropriate and accurate language called for in the coverage of "real" people with disabilities.

Scholarly research, advocates, and some of the aforementioned journalists, have continually asked the fictional media to not only add more characters with disabilities but change the light under which they are seen, for full and accurate inclusion. Few studies have called on news outlets to include more coverage of individuals with disabilities in the same way as they have called on the fictional media. However, the news media has not been given a full pass in regard to how often and how they portray individuals with a disability.

THE IMAGES OF DISABILITY IN THE POPULAR PRESS

While the images of disability in the popular press should be inherently different than what is seen in fictional media, there is quite a bit of overlap in the categorical analysis. The following is offered as a brief analysis of disability in the popular press (see Haller 2010 for a more in-depth look at news coverage of disability). The majority of images fall into either the *traditional* or *progressive* models of representation. The traditional model focuses on the individuals with disabilities different from others in society (Nelson 1994) and can be broken down into subcategories of *medical, supercrip, social pathology,* and Haller (1995) adds the *business* model. The *progressive* model focuses on how society deals with a population that includes those with disabilities (Nelson 1994) and can be broken down to the subcategories of a *minority/civil rights* model, *cultural pluralism*, and here Haller (1995) adds the *legal* and *consumer* models.

Much like its counterpart in fictional media (the victim), the *medical* model focuses on individuals with disabilities as dependent on health professionals for cures and/or maintenance. The implications in such stories are that disabilities are a problem to be solved and/or cured (Riley 2005). Gardner and Radel (1978) found that one half of news references to individuals with disabilities portrayed them as dependent and reliant on others. In more recent examinations, Englandkennedy (2008) found that journalistic coverage of Attention Deficit Disorder focuses on diagnosis, both the over- and mis- diagnosis, based on misinterpreting symptoms as well as the overuse of Ritalin. Holton, Farrell, and Fudge (2014) focused on journalists' coverage of autism, finding that newspapers focused more on "causes and potential cures" than any other aspects.

The *supercrip* (the hero) is represented as one that functions normally despite their disabilities or one that performs superhuman feats. These reports are usually focusing on the sensational value of the story rather than the accuracy of the representation (Barnes 1991). The important image to put forth is that of someone who can "overcome" their disability. Whether it is possible for others with the same disability to do the same is seemingly irrelevant. These narratives are typically drawn when the media covers athletes with a disability, in which someone has overcome such a disability to perform competitively (Hardin and Hardin 2004). Frequently the supercrip appears to be the subject in human interest stories showcasing someone (typically young and attractive individuals) with a visible disability performing an extraordinary feat. Dahl (1993) calls these "heroes by hype." She found that Canadian marathoners with disabilities were "packaged" for programs and publicity in a way that runners without disabilities were not, even though they were all running for charitable causes.

The *social pathology* or economic model (the fool) portrays individuals with disabilities as disadvantaged, looking to society for economic support. This model reports rights for individuals with disabilities as "gifts" or handouts. Additionally, some coverage still stereotypes individuals with disabilities as "strange" or "bizarre." This may come from the fact that individuals with disabilities are rarely part of the discussion of disability issues in the popular press. Particularly when it comes to cognitive disabilities, family and societal viewpoints are often highlighted and discussed over the viewpoints of those that have the disability (Holton et al., 2014). Renwick (2016) addresses the issue that the news media is completely controlled by journalists and editors, and when individuals with disabilities are readily available for interview they should be utilized and allowed to speak for themselves, yet they are not. We might also see celebrities without disabilities speaking on behalf of individuals with disabilities and offering to make personal sacrifices to help a particular charity or group (Barnes 1991). This coverage highlights the "need" for individuals without disabilities to provide handouts for those individuals with disabilities.

The *business* model seems to directly relate to the ADA and argues that media content may show accessibility as not profitable (Haller 1995). Thomas DeLeire (2000) in his article, "The Unintended Consequences of the Americans with Disabilities Act," breaks down the economic reality of the ADA. He reports on how individuals with disabilities have been negatively impacted, as a consequence of the ADA has been to decrease employment and employment opportunities for individuals with disabilities. Renwick and associates (2014) found that film representations of occupations for individuals with disabilities reflected some of this model as well. Individuals with disabilities were often seen in low-paying, low-skilled positions. While individuals with disabilities were employed, when attempting to move up in an organization or on to complex tasks, they were not given the support needed. This caused them to fail and ultimately harmed the business.

Moving to the progressive model, the *minority/civil rights* model is the first deviation from the fictional images of disability. This representation is one that highlights individuals with disabilities as members of a minority dealing with legitimate grievances (Clogston 1990). Reports often cover active demands for political change. While less frequent in the popular press, this coverage extends to discussions of the Americans with Disabilities Act and the importance of the rights provided within. Haller, Dorries, and Rahn (2006) credit media coverage of the policy with bringing disability rights before the general public (see also Haller 1995 for more information regarding news media and the Americans with Disabilities Act). Further coverage of policies or governmental processes in place spend less time representing the legitimacy of grievance and more on simple presentation of fact, such as whether budgets are being reduced, organizations defunded, and others. Similarly, the *legal* model presented by Haller (1995) focuses on the legality of treatment of individuals with a disability and the legal halting of discrimination.

Cultural pluralism portrays disability as just one aspect of a multifaceted individual, essentially bringing little attention to an individual's disability. The representation is the same or very similar to that of someone without a disability (Clogston 1990). Gardner and Radel (1978) report findings of one quarter of news items with individuals with disabilities as capable of being full members of society. This coverage would highlight the individual as independent and capable, whereas the majority of coverage found showed the opposite. Renwick (2016) might look to this type of representation as part of the "optimal" approach, as by depicting disability as one aspect of an individual the focus is on the person more than the disability, and here we may see more from that individual's perspective than in other approaches to media coverage. As journalists select the news frames they use to present their information, they provide meaning to their consumers which may impact a variety of dimensions of society. Finally, the *consumer* model taps into facets of how accessibility can be profitable to businesses (Haller 1995). Renwick and others (2014) again provide some example here with a fictional look at how when individuals with disabilities are employed they will not only shop but sometimes do so to excess and with abandon.

There has not been a lot of scholarly research examining the coverage of individuals with disabilities in the popular press alone (Holton et al., 2014). Much disability in the media research is designed to cover all media outlets for the widest cross-section of influence. There are ethical concerns directed at the news and journalists (see Starck 2001) regarding the coverage of individuals with disabilities (much of the press is blanketly criticized for potential negative effects on attitudes, beliefs, and behaviors of their consumers, Ferré 2009). However, this examination is most interested in examining how fictional characters with disability (with both actors with disabilities and without) are discussed within the press, and how these images are usually framed, and provides a specific analysis of the media coverage of one fictional character.

THE IMAGES OF "HOLLYWOOD" DISABILITY IN THE POPULAR PRESS

When looking specifically at media coverage of characters versus simply the actors that play them, nonfictional media has run the gamut of representation. Much like the fictional representations, there is very little coverage of characters with disabilities. In fact, one *Los Angeles Times* article even laments the underrepresentation in fictional media, headlining, "Disabled actors plead for a chance. Marlee Matlin and others say they have been ignored in Hollywood's recent campaign to diversify" (Anderson 2016). This article covering the Ruderman Studio-Wide Roundtable on Disability Inclusion, speaks strongly about the inclusion of the largest minority group in America, people with disabilities, and includes quotes from advocates seeking inclusion in fictional media. Additionally, discussion in the press focused on "disability drag," having actors without a noticeable disability playing characters with a disability.

Much like the fictional portrayal, these articles have predominantly fostered stereotypes of various disabilities. Some coverage has been positive and well-represented—for example, Mireya Navarro's 2007 article, "Clearly, Frankly, Unabashedly Disabled," covering reality television stars with disabilities such as *Last Comic Standing*'s Josh Blue. Navarro quotes Lawrence Carter-Long of the Disabilities Network of New York City, saying, "More people are saying, 'This is who I am. If you have a problem with it, that's your problem'" speaking of individuals with a disability in the media. Liz Gill (1992) in her article, "Shaking Off the Image Handicap" covers characters within advertisements, highlighting the perspective of Dr. Stephen Duckworth who is the founder of Disability Matters and a wheelchair user, focusing this article's attention on the perspective of those with disabilities versus other experts.[1] However, many articles have focused on the "idiot" characters or the article content has been insensitive to the fictional character, completely ignoring the *Disability Language Style Guide.*

In an article discussing "moronic siblings" the movie *Rainman* is discussed. Dustin Hoffman's character is clearly autistic but the report states, "If you are going to have an idiot brother, please let him be an idiot savant." (Collins and Furtado 2011)." Forrest Gump is said to have "glamourised gormlessness" as discussed in *The Financial Times* (Andrews 1994). Once again, this is a reference to a character with cognitive disabilities as very stupid or foolish. Further insensitivity is found in the *New York Times* in their discussion of Blair Underwood's portrayal of *Ironside* as someone that is "Disabled, But Still Dangerous: 'Ironside,' the Series Remake, Has Its Debut on NBC" (Genzlinger 2013) implying that a physical disability would normally prevent one from being an adequate opponent. Even in articles declaring a change in Hollywood with "more modern sensibility," characters may be seen as having to overcome their disability or that their quest to reach a goal such as independence is "courageous" ("The National" 2017). As mentioned, these reports of "Hollywood" disability are very similar to the coverage of "real" individuals with disabilities. But, does fictional character coverage fit the same model structure outlined earlier?

FRAMING OF FICTIONAL CHARACTERS WITH DISABILITIES

Unsurprisingly, the focus of the majority of articles discussing characters with a disability focus on the actor playing the character so both will be analyzed here. While most of the attention in this text is interested in the "character coverage," it is not unlikely that audiences often conflate the two (character and actor playing said character). In fact, a subset of media studies on parasocial interactions and relationships (see Dibble, Hartmann, and Rosaen's 2016 discussion of parasocial relationships for more) focuses on the idea that many viewers develop feelings and perceived relationships with characters and actors that may blur the line between fiction and reality. This is heightened by actors using social media as their characters and people feeling increases in interactions with celebrities through the same format. Schiappa, Gregg, and Hewes (2005) further this with their examination of the parasocial contact hypothesis which offers discussion regarding inclusion of intergroup contact which may be highlighted when bringing social media into the traditional mass media context.

Based on this blending, one might expect that the popular press would be full of accolades for the wonderful casting of diverse individuals or tackling complex problems such as disability, or perhaps even frank discussions regarding the falsehoods of such portrayals. What the popular press really looks like, however, is very limited in the coverage of characters with disabilities (which really isn't surprising given the lack of fictional characters with a disability as discussed in chapter 1) and most of these are in the same vein as the fictional portrayals, reiterating the stories of different or "abnormal," victim, or supercrip. However, does this coverage actually match more traditional coverage of disabilities in the media?

If we look at the traditional models of representation that focus on individuals with disabilities being different from others in society, we see many articles that present the other-ness of a character or actor first. Articles highlight the "disabled actor" or "disabled advocate" within discussions. Max, the character from *Parenthood*, discussed in chapter 1 is described in the article, "Making Drama Out of 'Ordinary Life' Can Be Murder," as demanding and as having insecure behavior and a need to control every situation (*The Times & Transcript* 2014). Following the medical model, Jocelyn Purdy (1989) reports on an actor/character that is an amputee as "disabled but going through their lives in a successful way," that the individual is "solving" their problem of being an amputee. The headline of Lawrie Masterson's 2010 article may say enough with "The blind leading the blonde?" as perhaps a flippant statement of disbelief that a lead character who is blind might be taking another under his wing? Michael J. Fox briefly returned to television with a sitcom character, also with Parkinson's, and Kennedy (2012) reports on his reliance on drugs to be able to return to the small screen.

Most of the popular press coverage of fictional characters with a disability seems to fall under the supercrip designation. Articles highlight individuals with disabilities as being "courageous," having "exceptionalities," and that "disability is no obstacle." RJ Mitte, the actor with cerebral palsy on *Breaking Bad*, is often referenced (or his character Walter White Jr.) as not allowing his disability to prevent him from acting (Strauss 2008) or (perhaps ironically) playing a character with cerebral palsy. Becky, the cheerleader on *Glee* with Down syndrome is also discussed as a role model for others with Down syndrome and can show them that "anything is possible" (Pemberton 2013). In perhaps the most "meta" of articles, Virginia Burrough's (2006) "Disability Hasn't Slowed Success of Marcus A. York; Former Area Resident Lands Guest Role in 'The Office'" is a human-interest story on how York, an actor in a wheelchair, landed a starring guest role on *The Office*. The "meta" of the article is that his character is on the program to teach the main characters about disability awareness.

There is very little coverage of characters with a disability falling under the social pathology model. One reason for this is likely that within fictional media, characters needing charity or economic support are not usually the main characters of a television program. They are predominantly seen as one-episode characters seeking aid from the regular cast. In movie character coverage, however, the closest example may be when Forrest Gump is described as "guileless" and "slow thinking" (Rea 1994). He is obviously presented as cognitively disabled, and this presentation of him as a fool is very similar to the aforementioned "idiotic" presentations. In what may be a spurious connection could be any seemingly flippant press coverage of a character that adds a demeaning adjective in their description of a character with a disability. The business model, when it comes to popular press coverage of characters with disabilities, is also limited; however, there is some discussion here on accessibility for actors/actresses with a disability and how it may be "costly" to use an actor with a disability in some roles (Rosenburg 2013).

At the time of this text's printing there were no real examples of coverage of a character within the minority/civil rights model. There are several articles, however, discussing the lack of representation of individuals with a disability in the media, calling for media versus political change. These articles all provide support for the grievances of those that are not represented. Woodburn and Ruderman (2016) in the *Los Angeles Times* provide a thorough breakdown of the lack of all minorities but focus on individuals with disabilities. They report that there has been improvement in representation for all minorities except for those with disabilities. The article provides an interesting breakdown of what the television landscape would look like if all minorities (females were included here as they are minorities in the TV landscape but not in the U.S.) were presented at the same percentage as those with disabilities and that "inequality of self-representation matters on a real, human level" (final paragraph).

Kennedy (2012) looks further into what industry organizations can do such as the Screen Actors Guild (SAG) and the Alliance for Inclusion in the Arts. Both of these organizations have been advocating for more research regarding the representation and inclusion of disability in the media as well as having more representation and accuracy in the media. Adam Moore, the Equal Employment Opportunity and Diversity Director of SAG-American Federation of Television and Radio Artists and Actors' Equity Association's (AFTRA), is quoted as saying, "If you don't see your family or what you look like or your experience reflected in the fictional environments—and more increasingly the real environments in reality television—if you don't see yourself reflected there, it reinforces this idea that you may not have the same place at the table of society that other people do" (Kennedy 2012, p. 2).

There is further media coverage of actors and characters that fit neatly into the cultural pluralism model, highlighting that an individual's disability is only one part of a multi-faceted character. When the television show *Switched at Birth* first came on the air the majority of coverage highlighted the fact that so many characters were deaf. In recent coverage, the focus is more on the drama contrived within the series and the numerous dimensions of the characters (Starr 2017) versus the deafness of the characters. While Strauss (2008) presented RJ Mitte as a supercrip, he also presents the character he plays as "just a teenager that happens to have cerebral palsy." Jane Lynch of *Glee* discusses her character's treatment of Becky, stating reserve in her first episode then realizing that her treatment of the character was not mean "she was treating her just like she would treat one of the other kids, because she knew that's the way Becky wanted to be treated: Like just another one of the kids." (Canwest News Service 2010, B1). The legal model, much like the business model, focuses mainly on the rights of actors with disabilities to play the characters with disabilities in the media, whereas there is little to no discussion regarding the consumer model.

While this has been just an overview of some of the media coverage of fictional characters with disabilities and how they are framed, what can also be important is the language used in the discussions, not just the adjectives or descriptors. When an article really focuses on dissecting a character with a disability, how does that analysis read? As it can sometimes be difficult to visualize what these guidelines may look like or how they may be used within an article, let us use *Ironside* and the *New York Times* 2013 article as an example on the coverage of a character with a disability in the media.

IRONSIDE: AN ANALYSIS

Again, Ironside[2] is a fictional character in a wheelchair played by the venerable actor, Blair Underwood. For this analysis guidelines adapted from the Research and Training Center on Independent Living by the Rocky Mountain Americans with Disabilities Association (2013) were used. These guidelines were established to help media professionals appropriately write about individuals with disabilities to "create a straightforward, positive view of people with disabilities" rather than an "insensitive portrayal that reinforces common myths and is a form of discrimination" (ADA Knowledge 2017). A breakdown of the guidelines follows:

Journalists should make sure to *put people first*[3]—the focus of a story should be on the individuals, not the disability. An individual is first and foremost a person and the focus should be on that fact versus focusing on a disability. This also includes the descriptive writing. Rather than saying "disabled actor/character" or addressing a specific disability with "deaf actor/character" the disability should come second (if it is needed at all), stating "the character with a disability" or "the character that is hard of hearing." The second guideline follows this idea—*do not focus on disability*. Unless something is crucial to a story, there should be more focus on quality of life than the downsides of disability. When discussing disability make sure to *avoid generic labels*—there is no group of "the disabled." Every individual with a disability is unique and should be addressed as such. Along these same lines, be sure to *avoid euphemisms*; this condescending language is often used when describing disability or individuals with disabilities such as "handicapable" or "physically inconvenienced."

Further guidelines address more than simply word choice. Journalists should *avoid sensationalizing*, adding the context of saying someone with a disability is "afflicted" or the "victim" of their disability. Similarly, disability is not synonymous with disease so *do not imply disease* such as referring to individuals as patients. Sometimes a long-term illness or injury does lead to a permanent disability—that does not, however, mean that the disability itself is a disease. When writing one should *emphasize abilities* of individuals with disabilities rather than focus on the limitation of a disability. For example, rather than focus on the fact that perhaps someone with a specific physical disability can't run a marathon in under three hours, focus on the fact that they can run a marathon. But, *do not portray people with disabilities as superhuman*, as has been discussed in this text as well as in previous research. There are a variety of potential negative effects in this area from raising false expectations to increasing negative treatment by others. Finally, while it seems simple, *maintain the integrity of each individual*, by not using offensive imagery or language. This factor is often overlooked in discussions of disability or individuals with disability.

To highlight these ideas let's examine the aforementioned article of Robert Ironside from the television show *Ironside* which comes from the *New York Times* article titled, "Disabled, But Still Dangerous: 'Ironside,' the Series Remake, Has Its Debut on NBC" by Neil Genzlinger from October 2, 2013. The article is a presentation and review of the character and pilot episode of the program (contrary to most work examining characters with disabilities that focus on the actor playing the role).

When examining the text, there are things that are done well, and others that are poorly constructed. The written review of the character of Ironside presents Ironside as a supercrip. However, this presentation is a bit more tongue in cheek, laughing at the TV program's representation of an individual in a wheelchair. "Ironside notices a gun under a cushion. 'How the hell did you see that?' another officer asks, marveling at the detective's magical powers." (Genzlinger 2013, C2). Even with the facetious presentation the article does little to dissuade the notion that Ironside is above and beyond in his abilities of a police officer.

The very first word of the title "Disabled, But Still Dangerous: 'Ironside,' the Series Remake, Has Its Debut on NBC" gives the first clue that this article is not about *putting people first*.[4] It is a discussion of a character with a disability and the entire *focus* of the review is on the fact that the main character is in a wheelchair. To give the author credit he does point out that the program is not "doing real people with disabilities any favors," yet, the entire review focuses on the disability for better or worse (while later criticizing the program for doing the same thing).

While the article does a nice job of referring to "people with disabilities," there is still some *generic labeling* when referring to "nondisabled officers" but no use of *euphemisms* in any references. The language of the articles does not *sensationalize* or *imply disease* but does very little to *emphasize abilities*. As most of the article is criticizing the program for its portrayal of Ironside, there is trivialization of Ironside's observations and techniques. As the aforementioned example of finding the gun under the cushion, why shouldn't

Ironside's unique position be valued by the other officers? While this may not reduce the *integrity* of the character, the article does not paint Ironside in a positive light. His strength, both physical and emotional, is a "message" to others and his observations are obvious to anyone with any intelligence.

As mentioned, the portrayal within the article leans more to the superhuman with language such as calling to rename the show "Ironside on Steroids" or calling the character "Disabled, but still Dangerous." Both highlight the strength of the character. The article also highlights the active nature of the character by reporting on his physical strength and when Ironside beats a suspect for information.

The article does avoid euphemisms and does not imply disease. And, while the article does represent Ironside as a supercrip, it also shows his active lifestyle throughout the text. However, the popular press article spends more time dismissing any possible positives of the character's abilities. Perhaps the most interesting finding is that the article really focuses on the disability. While the story of Ironside's disability may be crucial to the plot and storyline of the television program, the article spends most of its text referring to Ironside's disability and the presentation of such. Genzlinger even ends the article, "As independent as this new Ironside is, thanks to the plodding writing here, he is being defined by his disability, the exact opposite of what someone in his condition would want." The article coverage and his last comment are fairly typical of newspaper coverage as Holton and others (2014) and Renwick (2016) discussed, relying on a journalist's viewpoint of what someone in a wheelchair would want versus seeking out that viewpoint from someone in a wheelchair.[5]

This analysis is just one example, bringing together the suggested guidelines of reporting on individuals with disabilities with the "real life" coverage of a fictional world. One may question if this critique would have been the same had Ironside been played by an actor with a disability who uses a wheelchair. As previously mentioned, this idea of actors with disabilities playing the characters with the same disabilities has been frequently discussed in the popular press (as well as through other forms of media).

DISABILITY DRAG

The bottom line then is that the popular press, much like fictional media, appears to have limited coverage of "real" or fictional individuals with a disability. Coverage of fictional characters may be slightly more positive than of "real" individuals but both see an inordinate amount of supercrip narratives (Hardin and Hardin 2004). With all of this questionable exposure on the audience separately (fictional and popular press) the next chapter looks at what might happen when these are put together.

NOTES

1. A remark has to be made, however, that Gill's headline includes the phrase "image handicap" but later in her article she directly discusses that the term handicap may be offensive.

2. The article on *Ironsides* is simply being used as an example of how the guidelines may be used or overlooked by newspapers from the editors to the authors of the text.

3. There is debate within disability communities regarding the use of people-first versus identity-first language. This discussion is further noted in chapter 3. For the purposes of examining the newspaper articles in this context, however, the text continues to follow the journalistic guidelines noted.

4. Yes, the writers don't always come up with the headlines; however, as the lead-in to the story it is describing what is within the text and is important to note with the larger example.

5. For the sake of being thorough, I did check to make sure that Genzlinger did not in fact regularly use a wheelchair.

Chapter Three

Image Echoes

Popular Press Coverage of Media Disability

Chapters 1 and 2 focused on representations of disability in fictional media and popular press separately. As noted, there have been several works looking at these two areas and the impact they each may have on individuals with disabilities as well as society overall. What is less discussed is the concept of "image echoes" or portrayals of a fictional character with a disability that is echoed in the popular press. The mere exposure effect (Zajonc 1968) states that the more we are exposed to a stimulus the more likely we are to feel a positive affect toward that stimulus. One condition, however, seems to be that the first exposure is not explicitly negative (Zajonc, 2001). A question, however, is what if the stimuli or images seen are more implicitly negative? What if one is seeing an inaccurate or a negative picture of disability on television and then sees reinforcement of that idea in the popular press?

Let's take, for example, the television program *Family Guy*. In 2010, the program introduced a character, Ellen, a high school student with Down syndrome for a date on one episode with one of the main characters, Chris. Ellen's character was pushy and demanding on the date and the character of Chris admits that he asked her out as he thought people with Down syndrome were different. While some viewers of the program debated the positivity or negativity of the portrayal, one prominent figure took the episode to heart and publicly commented on the show. Former Alaska Governor Sarah Palin criticized the show for the portrayal, accusing them of making fun of her son, Trig, and essentially, individuals with Down syndrome. Further, Palin and *Family Guy* producers engaged in heated public press discussions regarding the portrayal. Gail Williamson, executive director of the Down Syndrome Association at that time, argued within the popular press that you have to

29

take the bad with the good when it comes to full inclusion (Itzkoff 2010). However, some research has found that negative exposure has actually increased prejudice of minorities (Cole, Arafat, Tidhar, Tafesh, and Fox 2003). If these images do have the power to influence an audience as previous research has shown us, particularly within social cognitive and cultivation analysis research, what role might these image echoes have in influencing personal identity or one's sense of self?

As we have seen, representations of disability in both fictional media and popular press have been scarce, predominantly negative, and even positive or "supercrip" portrayals have been questionable. Very little research has been conducted to examine the potential role that reinforcement between fictional media and popular press may play on an audience. To examine these image echoes further it is important to understand the theoretical underpinnings of the effect of the media.

SOCIAL COGNITIVE THEORY

One of the founding theories within communication research is the social cognitive theory. Social cognitive theory (Bandura 1986) looks at how behavior modeling may transmit attitudes, values, and even behaviors from a source to a receiver. There is a wide field of study in this area examining the impact of the media in behavioral modeling. Much of this is discussed as media consumers are active participants that engage in reflecting and learning from the content consumed. According to Bryant (1990), "people use television's characters, stories, themes, jokes, and jargon in order to help facilitate conversations at home, work, school, and other arenas" (62). Fictional television programs contain an abundant number of images and ideas that people use in daily interpersonal interactions. Viewers that are learning about disability from the media take this new 'knowledge' to others. The media is used as a reference point for explanations or illustrations in conversations (Bryant 1990). Studies have indicated the pervasiveness of the media in the fact that most of these conversations take place away from the television viewing area. After all, do you need to discuss what you just watched with someone in the room or do you have the conversation later with someone that you didn't view a program with at that time? These conversations and group settings can foster peer support and supplement behavior change (Blase and Kerr 2000).

At an even more basic level, the media are used as common reference points to explain or justify certain points of view. Even with this, it would be wrong to suggest that public understandings of an issue are simply a result of viewing a particular program, as if this occurs in isolation. The inclusion of popular press exposure may increase its "social currency," people's willingness to reiterate what they have read or seen, and the value of information or a specific story in a social context (Kitzinger 1999). Their take-aways from a television program are no longer seen as only their personal commentary when the popular press reports on the same elements or findings.

An important element of social cognitive theory is the response-reinforcement of behaviors. If one is exposed to a behavior through television viewing and that behavior is accepted by others and those behaviors are reinforced, the behavior is more likely to be learned by others. While this is frequently discussed in the media to consumer/society aspect prior to behavior learning, the popular press can play the role of societal reinforcer for some content, particularly in scenarios where direct exposure may be limited. For example, if someone sees a television character with a disability being marginalized by others, everyone on television accepts this as normal behavior. Then the popular press also discusses the character in a stereotypical, demeaning manner, so the behavior of stereotyping individuals with disabilities is learned. (e.g., Max is autistic, Max is made fun of and shunned by kids his age on a television program. A newspaper article discussing the character as "troubled," "dangerous," or "problematic" and viewers/readers may be more apt to learn that someone with autism should be avoided.) Dillon, Byrd, and Byrd (1980) expressed this concern as well, "Unfortunately, a large number of programs depict disability in a manner that is disparaging to the disabled person. The same type of portrayal may be seen over and over again, thus contributing to a multiple modeling and reinforcing situation" (67). This is similar to advertising research that examines the impact of repeating messages, particularly for messages that are processed on a more peripheral level (shallow level) versus those that may be more important to the viewer (Nordhielm 2002).

Chen, Feng, and Leung (2014) address the media as a "major source" of information from which children, in particular, "learn and form their social views" (430). Further research has shown that patterns of behavior within the media are incorporated as they are believed to be what occurs in the real, non-mediated environment (Byrd 1989). In the context of disability in the media, social cognitive theory has been used to examine how media portrayals may influence attitudes of viewers about individuals with disabilities. For example, Chen and others (2014) found social learning effects from the presentation of both positive and negative media presentations of disabilities (to positive and negative attitudes toward disability, respectively) and further that media channels had a direct effect in this process; also significant in the process is interpersonal discussions regarding disability. But as noted in the study, few individuals could point out who they might discuss disabilities with in their lives. Social cognitive theory could also extend to the perceived treatment of those with disabilities by others. If a viewer is learning about a disability through the media and if the representation is negative, the media can impact attitudes toward those with disabilities and foster the negative treatment of individuals with disabilities in "real life" (Worrell and Zoller 2004). Byrd (1989) also presents the idea of negative behaviors toward individuals with disabilities on television being learned by viewers such that, "inappropriate behavior toward a person with a disability presented on television might provide the conditions for that behavior being learned by the viewer" (37).

When extending this further into the reinforcement of ideas, the addition of popular press coverage adds a layer not often examined within the media. Much of the social cognitive/learning process looks at one "model" of a behavior (one portrayal) and the impact on individuals. As these effects have been substantially supported (see Bandura 2001, for more in this area), we must consider the implications of the image echo and the double exposure that may be present for some media consumers. If a stereotypical or negative image is presented in fictional media and then reinforced with a stereotypical or negative image in the popular press, the impact may be even more substantial than with one source alone. Further, an additional role the popular press may play is that of presenting what a viewer may believe as the social norms regarding an issue. The theory of reasoned action addresses how these norms may influence behavior as well.

THEORY OF REASONED ACTION

The theory of reasoned action (Fishbein and Ajzen 1975) has been used to predict behavioral intentions (the step before behavioral change). This theory has been particularly used to provide a theoretical foundation for applied research within health communication and the impact of messages from peers as well as television and other forms of mass media (Roberts 1982). The theory of reasoned action posits that attitudes and subjective norms are the two factors that influence an individual's intention to change behavior (Ajzen and Fishbein 1980). Attitudes consist of feeling in favor of or against a particular behavior (Ajzen and Fishbein 1980). Fishbein and Ajzen (1975) also suggest that attitudes are learned and that the media can provide the information that leads to a certain disposition toward an individual with a disability. The theory posits that individuals who feel favorably about a behavior are more likely to intend to engage in that behavior in the future.

Subjective norms are people's perceptions regarding the extent to which specific others would approve of behavioral intentions (Ajzen and Fishbein 1980; Wong and Tang 2001), and represent the social pressures put on an individual to perform or not perform a certain behavior (Ajzen and Fishbein 1980). There are two specific components that comprise subjective norms—normative beliefs and motivation to comply. Normative beliefs are the individual's perceptions concerning their family's and friends' beliefs with regard to whether or not the individual should perform a particular behavior. How much an individual is driven to behave as they think others want them to act is their motivation to comply (Ajzen and Fishbein 1980). If we feel that important others want us to engage in a particular behavior and we are strongly motivated to behave as others want us to act, the theory of reasoned action predicts that our intentions to perform the behavior will increase.

According to this literature, the media has an indirect influence on attitudes. However, previous research in this area is mostly limited to marketing and political persuasion (Ajzen and Fishbein 1980; Gill, Grossbart, and Laczniak 1988). Notably, although this work has not been fully extended to entertainment media, logic from previous theory of reasoned action research showing how stimuli influence attitudes (e.g. Gillmore, Archibald, Morrison, and Wilsdon 2002) can be used to show how a media character's position on a behavior can influence viewer attitudes. For example, within disability research, scholars like Cumberbatch and Negrine (1992) found that characters without a disability showed different (negative) attitudes toward characters with disabilities more so than toward characters without disabilities. Characters with disabilities were treated with pity, fear, and patronizing attitudes and those without were treated with respect and attention. If exposure to this plays a role in shaping viewer attitudes, negative attitude change could be expected, whereas positive attitude change or reinforcement should occur for viewers if they perceive a character as having a positive attitude toward a behavior (treating characters with a disability the same as those without) (Ajzen and Fishbein 1980). Therefore, perceptions of a character's attitudes seem integral to the formation of a person's own attitudes about a behavior.

According to Smith, Nathanson, and Wilson (2002), realistic portrayals in the media may be perceived as not only more believable but also more relevant to viewers, heightening the probability of learning. In general, when viewers perceive television content as an accurate representation, they are more likely to be influenced (Fujioika, 1999). As media consumers may not have much direct experience with individuals with disabilities and the popular press is often seen as a realistic view into society, this presentation may increase viewers' perceptions of the normative beliefs regarding disability. If one believes these image echoes accurately represent how others may feel about individuals with disabilities, stereotyping and stigmatization may be perceived as normal. Of course, amount of exposure may also play a role, both directly and indirectly through the media.

CULTIVATION THEORY

Cultivation theory (Gerbner, Gross, Morgan, Signorielli, and Shanahan 2002) states that heavy viewers of television will believe that the "real" world more closely resembles what they see on television. If this is true, then television fills a void in one's direct experience. Shrum, Wyer, and O'Guinn (1998) suggest that viewers come "to 'cultivate' information they view on television by integrating it into their perceptions of real-world phenomena" (447). Viewers believe what they see as a reflection of the world or society. Cultivation is not static or linear but it is a continuous process of interaction between messages and contexts, a continuous exchange between viewers and what they are viewing (Gerbner, Gross, Morgan, and Signorielli 1994). The largest concern/discussion within cultivation seems to be that when an individual views a program on a regular basis they will begin to view the "real" world as similar to the world shown in the media.

To examine how this might work, Moy and Pfau (2000) present the cultivation paradigm, with its cultural indicators approach, as a way to explain the influence of television programming on perceptions of reality. They posit that the mass media serve as a powerful source of perceptions. In time, television, through the repetition of patterns, alters one's images and/or perceptions of "the ways of the world." These perceptions may most significantly impact viewers with limited direct experiences. The cultivation theory explains that whenever real and mediated reality converge they act to "resonate and amplify" each other, which produces a reinforcing affect. When individuals are unable to receive direct experience of situations or particular diversities they tend to accept the media's depictions of reality. If the media present them inaccurately, individuals may develop distorted perceptions of reality.

This process of mass media influence is termed "mainstreaming," which explains how heavy media use can "reduce or override differences in perspectives and behavior" from other sources, such as experiences or interpersonal exchanges, resulting in "shared meanings in people" (Moy and Pfau 2000). As a result, people who share common media experiences (especially across platforms such as television, newspapers or through social media) eventually come to view the world much as the media depict it. While yet to be directly examined, and most of cultivation research examines one form of media (usually television) at a time, the cross-platform image echoes are a significant example of increased exposure to an issue. The addition of social media as a third platform is further discussed in chapter 4.

If underrepresentation within fictional and popular press can impact attitudes of consumers (particularly those with no direct experience with an individual with a disability), this can lead viewers to believe that all individuals with disabilities are like the ones they see in the media. The lack of representation can lead one to believe that individuals with disabilities are "alone" or that these individuals are unimportant in the eyes of society. When it comes to negative or stereotypical presentations, the concern commonly reported is that heavy television viewers would not only be more likely to believe what they are seeing regarding disability (Diefenbach and West 2007) but that this belief would turn into fostering negative stereotypes toward those with disabilities. Stereotyping and stigmatization of individuals is not new and is frequently done in the "real" world on a regular basis. If the fictional media already resonates and amplifies these perceptions, having these issues reinforced with popular press coverage would make them even more salient to consumers. But, some theory exists that may alter the perception or impact of repeated exposures.

MERE EXPOSURE EFFECT

Within media examinations, much of mere exposure research focuses on advertising and how repetition impacts brand recognition (Baker 1999; Duff and Faber 2011). A psychological phenomenon, the mere exposure effect states that people tend to develop a preference for things merely because they are familiar with them (also sometimes called the familiarity principle) (Zajonc 2001). Bornstein and D'Agostino (1994) discuss mere exposure as an extremely well researched, two-step process. First, repeated exposure to a stimulus will increase perceptual fluency, an ease in processing the information. Secondly, the repeated exposure will increase positive feelings toward the stimulus. Based on this mere exposure theorists might state that the repeated exposure itself is more important for facilitating positive feelings than what the stimulus actually portrays.

If, as Duff and Faber (2011) theorize, liking is due to the "drop in negative initial avoidance reactions" (52) one might have with some unfamiliar stimuli (a disability in some instances), this may counter the previously discussed cultivation effects due to lack of direct experience, particularly when viewing a negative representation of an individual with a disability. If someone is not viewing a program to directly learn about a disability and they are repeatedly exposed to a regular character with a disability and there is the additional exposure of seeing that character/actor covered in the popular press, one should feel they are becoming familiar with the disability and any potentially negative reactions should be mitigated.

However, little research has been done examining specific and negative repetition (the theory posits that novel stimuli themselves are in fact negative in their novelty). If one has no knowledge of a disability, is exposed to repeated negative messages, would exposure itself be enough to start a positive frame or does the representation need to be positive? While advertisements don't frequently contain negative messages about the product being sold, research here is scarce. Outside of advertising specific messages, Roberts and Gettman (2004) did find that women exposed to more negative, self-objectifying words rated higher negative emotions then those exposed to messages of body empowerment. Their results support that exposure to negative messages within the media can increase a negative emotion within media consumers. Of course, much of this discussion may depend on how much attention media consumers are fully giving to the messages presented.

So, would most consumers of the *Family Guy* content see the jokes made at the character's expense and the representation differently as they are not thinking as deeply about individuals with Down syndrome as someone with direct experience, such as Palin? Palin has more direct experience with an individual that has Down syndrome; therefore, she would more critically process the information. If so, would the image echo of popular press's representation continue a more positive feeling toward individuals with Down syndrome for the "lighter" thinkers? As it seems research is inconclusive in this generalized area, we can look at the more individualized sense of self where the media has been found to have an impact on media consumers.

SENSE OF SELF

A few studies have examined the influence of fictional imagery on the personal identity of individuals with disabilities. The 2006 study that Heather Zoller and I conducted, examined the influence of the portrayal of multiple sclerosis (MS) on the program *The West Wing* on individuals with MS, finding that the disability was inaccurately portrayed and subsequently participants felt this affected their perception of self as well as how others viewed them. Zhang and Haller (2013) in a study examining people with diverse disabilities, found that the effect on identity was tied to whether individuals felt the image portrayed was positive or negative. Positive portrayals (regardless of accuracy) led to confirmation of their disability identity; however, negative portrayals led to a denial of their disability identity. As previously mentioned, one can also bring in the discussion of semantics when discussing disability at this point. How individuals with disabilities identify themselves also may play a role in language preferences. For individuals that put their disability first on how they identify, they are often more comfortable with identity first language (e.g., autistic person), whereas others that may not as strongly identify with their disability place person first language as a preference (e.g., person with autism). Thus far, there has not been a definitive agreement on preferences within disability language (see Dunn and Andrews 2015 for further discussion regarding professional adoption).

As was mentioned in chapter 2, the best thing to do when unsure how to refer to an individual with a disability is to simply ask their preference.

One's perception of self is a constructed organization of attributes, feelings, and identifications that a person takes as defining him or herself (Charmaz 1998a). Schroeder and Zwick (2004) discuss Foucault's ideas on the nature of being and sense of self and the imposition of limits and that these limits "restrict the set of possibilities open to self-formation" (28). Taken together these ideas highlight the fact that when one is discovering their personal identity many factors are taken into consideration to broaden one's view but there are also limits in place that may not allow an individual to fully realize their own sense of self. When it comes to individuals with disabilities they are already entering the social arena with different perspectives than those without disabilities (Murphy 1998). Their bodies are altered and the way they think of themselves and about the social world has been transformed. "One of my earliest observations was that social relations between the disabled and the able-bodied are tense, awkward, and problematic" (Murphy 1998, 63). Visible disability invites rude questions and remarks about difference. Invisible disability prompts accusations about failure to meet expectations. People with disabilities can find themselves being betrayed, stigmatized, exploited, and demeaned (Charmaz 1998a).

The sense of self of individuals with disabilities can also change once they realize how others view them. Altered social interaction can cause individuals to reassess themselves and their lives. This can lead to negative interpretations of self and how one appears to other people. Fictional and popular press images of disability hold up such a lens by allowing individuals with disabilities a glimpse at how others may perceive them. The processing of such information for individuals with disabilities may also play a role. According to Petty and Cacioppo (1986) and the elaboration likelihood model, those involved in a topic will inspect a message more closely (take a central route to processing), whereas individuals not involved may take a more peripheral route, paying less attention to the actual message conveyed. Within the central route, individuals with the ability and motivation to think about a topic will actively participate in processing a message. Those in the peripheral route lack the motivation or ability to fully process a message so other cues will be used to make a decision, such as the sender's attractiveness or credibility regarding an issue (e.g., a handsome actor seeming to have a disability; a credible story in a respected news outlet). As such, two things may occur: one, an individual with a disability will find flaws in an inaccurate presentation and dismiss it as ineffectual, or two, the increased attention will allow for a more significant impact of a message on one's sense of self or how others perceive individuals with a disability.

So, are these images "echoes" or are the representations within fiction and the popular press different enough to portray disabilities in a contrasting light? If individuals have more consumption options in the portrayals of their own disabilities to attend to, will they be able to more fully realize their own identity? But, how can one fully compare a fictional representation of a character from a televised series or movie with a nonfictional account of said character or the actor portraying the character? One way is for a more thorough analysis of what these echoes may be presenting.

IMAGE ECHOES AND THEORY

Let's look at two representations of disability that have been examined separately within fictional media and the popular press. As previously mentioned, in 2012 I conducted a large content analysis examining the portrayal of disability in fictional media (across a five-year sample of top-rated television programs). Findings from this study were largely in support of earlier work finding limited, negative, inaccurate portrayals. If we just look at the findings related to cognitive disabilities, we will find that although there were more cognitive disabilities found than physical disabilities, the combination of the two were still well below U.S. census numbers (11%). As was discussed earlier, negative language is predominantly used to describe individuals with cognitive disabilities, such as crazy or psychotic. Individuals with cognitive disabilities were seen more as criminals, surly, troubled, socially awkward and in need of guidance or help throughout episodes.[1] As this was fictional media one would expect more accurate/positive findings in the same time period within actual news coverage.

Holton and others (2014) in their examination of autism coverage within the news thoroughly examine the broader cognitive disability news media coverage. While it may take a precipitating event for a journalist to cover a cognitive disability (such as the now debunked theory of vaccinations leading to autism), this does not mean an increase in understanding. As previously mentioned, news coverage of cognitive disabilities often does not include the viewpoint of those with cognitive disabilities, leading to impartial and frequently stigmatizing coverage of disabilities. The use of stigmatizing language may suggest to media consumers that an individual with a disability should be avoided, that they are not normal. Holton and partners also point out the numerous studies that have found news coverage of cognitive disabilities to be equated with "violence, danger, instability, and hopelessness" (192).

These two examinations of cognitive disability within the media, fiction and news, highlight the concerns regarding image echoes presented earlier. If we look at some of the theories and concepts discussed, we can deconstruct these ideas a bit further. The presentation of cognitive disability in fictional and news media has been found to be infrequent, stigmatizing, and overwhelmingly negative. With just the fictional portrayal, social cognitive theory would present concern for behavioral modeling and cultivation theory would say individuals exposed to these presentations take away the idea that individuals with cognitive disability in real life are akin to what viewers are being exposed to within the media. Add to that the news portrayal and the connection to normative beliefs and one is being hammered again that individuals with cognitive disabilities, particularly mental illnesses, are dangerous and should be stigmatized (see figure 3.1). Further, as these ideas continue to grow amongst viewers, there is nothing slowing down the social construction of stigmatization of individuals with cognitive disabilities.

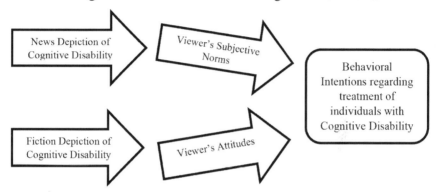

Figure 3.1. Graphical representation of media's impact and the theory of reasoned action

Rethinking the negative trend of the coverage of cognitive disability, if mere exposure effect holds, the limited portrayals alone would not increase positive perceptions of individuals with a disability, but repeated exposure across platforms may cause a drop in the audience reaction for individuals that believe the stereotypes associated with individuals with a disability. Of course, it is unclear if the *type* of portrayals will play a role here, but it would be relatively safe to hypothesize that increased exposure to positive representations in both fictional and popular press coverage would lead to familiarity and positive perceptions of a previously unknown health issue. All of these theoretical foundations also play a role in the sense of self for an individual with a disability which will be discussed more fully later in the text. Prior to that, however, this text would be remiss if it did not at least briefly look at another platform of possible echoes—social media.

NOTE

1. While this more recent example found highlights supporting the previous research, I did want to point out a foundational study that was even more thorough and specific with its analysis. Wahl and Roth (1982) had 85 volunteers examine 385 television programs from 1981

to examine both references to the cognitive disability of mental illness and characters or a portrayal of mental illness (only if clearly labeled in the program). Coders also rated whether they would use any of 10 positive or 10 negative adjectives provided in describing the characters. Their findings showed that the 35 persons labeled to be cognitively disabled as mentally ill tended to be "single males with no specified occupation . . . with a mean age of 40" (604). While some of the positive adjectives were used by coders such as "loyal" and "friendly," these were heavily outweighed by the negative descriptors such as "confused," "aggressive," and "dangerous." Further the study points out that most of the characters were identified only by their mental illness with no real social identity outside of that scope presented. Their findings "confirm the fears of mental health professionals that negative stereotyping of mentally ill persons is prevalent in prime-time television programming" (606).

Chapter Four

Additional Echoes

Mobile and Social Media Presentations of Disability

While this text is primarily focused on fictional television with the popular press role in image echoes, one would be remiss if there was no discussion of the possibilities from social media and mobile technologies. There have been significant changes throughout the time periods mentioned in the beginning of this text in how media content is delivered, accessed, viewed, shared, and utilized by an audience, which presents unique challenges and opportunities for various populations. This brief chapter will focus specifically on three ideas; new ways of viewing content and mobile technologies, then social media which have individuals with disabilities as generators and consumers of content, and in particular how this may play a role in shaping identity and/ or stigmatization. This chapter also speaks to these further echoes and the potentials that exist with new technologies reinforcing or helping to negate some of the previously mentioned effects.

As use of technology continues to grow and we become more reliant on having information at our fingertips, we might expect that new and mobile technology would have a positive impact on educating a population regarding a topic they know little about.

Unfortunately, if people do not recognize a gap in their own knowledge, they are less likely to seek out information to supplement what they see in fictional media. So, if I see information on a television show and believe it or think little about its veracity, I am unlikely to seek out further information across other media platforms.

Television consumers spend on average four hours a day watching television (Nielsen Total Audience Report Q4 2016). That number is continuing to increase thanks to our ability to view television via various technologies from streaming Netflix to mobile TV subscriptions (Nielsen 2015). When adding in non-streaming content (e.g., Blu-Rays) that number continues to increase by, according to Nielsen 2015, at least 10 minutes per day. Digital technologies have increased accessibility for individuals through enhanced closed captions, audio descriptions, clean audio, and not to mention the mobile capabilities of viewing media through various screens and smartphones.

NEW AND MOBILE TECHNOLOGIES

As we know, there are multiple ways for individuals to interact with television and popular press content. New mobile technologies have afforded individuals a lot more options when it comes to the consumption of media. We can watch television from anywhere, connect with news, family or friends at virtually any time. We consume professionally created content or more user-generated materials. Thus far, research on these diverse ways of viewing content has shown that while immersion or presence, "communication in a mediated environment with some varying feeling of non-mediation" (Westerman and Skalski 2010, 64), may be impacted by image size (see Rigby, Duncan, Cox and Gould 2016 for more) there is little to no research on the role this may play on direct or indirect effects, specifically on individuals with disabilities.

Some research has examined information processing from small/mobile devices versus large screen use. For example, Kim and Sundar (2016) found that individuals viewing content with an advertisement on a small-screen smartphone formed "greater cognitive trust in the ad than those exposed to large-screen smartphone and video ads" (58). Trust formed utilizing less cognitive demand, affective (enjoyment and satisfaction) trust, was found to be greater for larger screens. These findings also go back to the discussion of how we process information, heuristically or systematically, more peripherally or centrally. Kim and Sundar found that individuals using a small screen processed information more systematically/analytically than those viewing the larger screens.

As was discussed in chapter 3, how individuals process health information regarding disability has not been fully examined, therefore it is difficult to determine, precisely, the impact of screen size and viewing media through mobile devices on individuals with disabilities. Some research has shown that personally relevant health messages will be more systematically processed (see Quintero Johnson, Harrison and Quick 2013), therefore it would make sense that those with a disability will participate in more systematic message processing of media content regarding their own or a similar disability. It is quite possible then that small screen size, such as mobile viewing, may impact those with disabilities more strongly than when viewed through a more traditional medium. (Again, as research here is still un-founded, the above is based more on educated connections versus empirical research.)

While at least 80% of U.S. adult internet users have searched online for health information, there are also online forums to provide social support, and mobile technology being used for health promotion campaigns (Hu 2015). There is quite a bit of research devoted to mhealth or the use of mobile technology to support public health and care, particularly in the case of interventions for the spreading of communicable diseases or health man-agement in the case of mhealth apps (Matias and Sousa 2017; Singh et al 2016). The use of new and mobile technologies for health promotion cam-paigns has been commended as they may help to decrease the gaps between individuals with low and high health literacy. However, for individuals with a disability, accessing technology for the gathering of health information, viewing content, or interacting with others may be challenging. Aside from direct barriers such as captions or voice reading, some caregivers and family members may ban certain sites or heavily monitor technology use (Caton and Chapman 2016).

Aside from the simple ability to access information, the growth of social media and social networking sites provides even further avenues to exposure to health information and individuals' perceptions of health. People seek and provide support by participating in forums and communities such as those found in social media (Hu 2015). According to Ytre-Arne (2016) and her look at bloggers with myalgic encephalomyelitis, internet forums have been positioned to try and affect research funding as well as political attention. Furthering the sense of self and managing identity within these contexts was important for her participants. The capabilities new technology has given individuals with illness or disability have been found to play a role in how individuals rethink their sense of self. This is "not merely relevant for the individual, it also refers to and potentially challenges dominant discourses of what it means to participate in society" (Ytre-Arne 2016, 68). Social media is one area that offers individuals with a disability the communication tools necessary to participate in managing their identity and potentially others' view of a disability. Social media has also been used as a learning platform for knowledge generation and science communication (Hemsley and Dann 2014).

SOCIAL MEDIA USE: GENERATING AND CONSUMING CONTENT

While digital technology *may* alter how individuals process health informa-tion viewed across platforms, there have been studies to support the fact that social media use does in fact impact individuals with disabilities (Caton and Chapman 2016). Social media is unique from traditional forms of media in that most information is created or shared by users of the websites. Information received often seems to be coming from friends, family, or organizations that one is affiliated with usually by choice. Searches for information can lead one down a rabbit hole of discussions and debates surrounding a variety of topics.

When I type "disability" into the search bar on Facebook, it is interesting to see the number of pages that pop up offering services or support for individuals with a disability, or news regarding disability for me to follow. The groups to join include discussion and support groups, marketplaces for medical equipment, or just areas for making new friends. When I see my friends' posts I am gratified to see those with disabilities posting about "owning" their disability or advocating for their rights and the rights of others. Even the top public posts look positive toward individuals with a disability, dismay over a family being denied services to their child with a disability, or discussions about extra costs to those individuals with disabilities.

Social media can fulfill a variety of needs for individuals. Individuals can seek and share health information, provide support, receive support, spread awareness of health issues and advocate for policy or organizational change (Hu 2015). For some individuals with disabilities the use of the social media has aided in the development of building relationships as well as their own personal identity (Caton and Chapman 2016). Shpigelman and Gill (2014), in their article "Facebook Use by Persons with Disabilities" found that individuals with disabilities use Facebook much as individuals without disabilities do for strengthening ties with others, and to increase their social capital (ability to participate with larger groups). Interestingly, they also found that individuals with disabilities were more likely to use Facebook to connect with and build relationships with friends and groups without disabilities than with their friends and groups with a disability.

Part of the discussion of relationship building within social media also comes back to privacy concerns and issues. While some social media sites allow for strict privacy controls regarding who has access to content, not all users know about the features or are able to use them. Therefore, discussing disability issues online can be frightening for some, as others may not be aware of their disability or they may be concerned what other members of the public (e.g., future employers) might think (Shpigelman and Gill 2014). Further, concerns exist regarding the potential for bullying within social media when too many people have access to information provided.

SOCIAL MEDIA SHAPING IDENTITY AND STIGMATIZATION

Recent research has found that social media use can have an impact on media content and producers. While this has been found more with popular press media, for example the reporting on the #CripTheVote hashtag coverage in the popular press,[1] there is still potential for change within fictional media. While Hu (2015) found that there is not a lot of empirical research examining ehealth advocacy, anecdotal evidence suggests that online petitions and calls across social media sites such as Twitter have not only advocated for health-related causes but have changed health policies. This form of advocacy, along with social media support possibilities may play a role in providing positive "echoes" that will affect identity and/or social construction of disability and stigmatization. On the other end of the spectrum, "inspiration porn" and the use of social media to share imagery of individuals with disabilities doing something "ordinary" as a part of a meme to motivate others has been found to perpetuate stereotypes and the objectification of individuals with disabilities (Gagliardi 2017). Much like the discussion of traditional media, without empirical research into the impact of social media on identity and further stigmatization, much of what we can discuss is speculation and educated guesses based on communication theory and health information research.

While the echoing effects of technology and social media may not be as precise as those between traditional television and popular press, one can see how individuals may still be exposed to multiple, cross-platform messages relaying the same information. This is not to suggest that the order of events would be: see a character with a disability on television, read an article about that character, then follow that character on Twitter. While this would be the most linear process of echoing, what is more likely to be true is that there is some level of exposure to messages regarding disability within traditional media and online sources. Individuals exposed to these cross-platform messages may be attending to messages more closely and therefore be more likely to be affected by that exposure.

Going back to that linear example: if one is presented with all accurate, positive messages regarding a disability, regardless of platform, it would make sense that individuals with disabilities would continue to build positive personal identities and those without disabilities would form more positive attitudes about said disability. If presented with all inaccurate, negative messages, individuals with a disability will begin to have a poor sense of self and personal identity and there is a good chance that those without a disability will be more likely to have negative attitudes and stigmatize individuals with the disability presented. Mixed messages across the board are likely to have mixed results. If I have a disability, view content on a small-screen smartphone (which increases my cognitive trust), and then see that disability representation reinforced in popular media, BUT my social media network presents only positive images, which presentation is most likely to impact my identity? For individuals that don't have a particular disability, it is impossible, without more empirical research, to determine which medium is more likely to play the strongest echo if there are mixed messages. But we can be relatively certain that the echoes would still take place and have an impact.

This brief look at technology and social media use by individuals with disabilities was simply to touch on possibilities of further image echoes and the potential of new technologies to reinforce or negate effects from more traditional forms of media. For a more in-depth look into social media and disability, I recommend the book *Disability and Social Media: Global Perspectives* edited by Katie Ellis and Mike Kent. The text is an in-depth examination of social media and disability areas such as access, engagement, community, and advocacy. While these echoes may be less examined and currently concerning than those within the popular press, section two looks specifically at what the media is doing and how the media has been found to impact viewers and society when it comes to the portrayals of disability within the media.

NOTE

1. See the *Washington Post* article "The 2016 Conversation has Ignored Disabled People, Now They Want to be Heard" from February 10, 2016, for an example of how #CripTheVote was covered in the press.

II

What Is the Media Doing?

Remember those hundreds of studies and thousands of hours viewed to see what the media is showing and our concern about the effects on viewers? Most of the research here is focused on whether someone is going to become more violent or promiscuous from watching the media. After all, these are pretty empirical, measurable ideas—see someone being violent on television, go off and hit someone in real life, count the hits, see the effect. Okay, maybe they aren't all that easy to research but these are more tangible ideas to offer society. More sex viewed = more sex performed, versus more intrinsic, less empirical behaviors. For instance, how is the media impacting how individuals treat others? Are people stereotyping and stigmatizing others more due to representations in the media? What impact does the media have on our identities and how we construct our meanings of self? Examining and researching these areas can be challenging as you may be asking people to think of their own undesirable behaviors or to report on doing things that are not socially desirable.

The following section deals with these questions in two ways, first by examining the impact of the representation of physical disabilities followed by cognitive disabilities. Each of these discussions is followed by case studies of primary research examining individuals that are deaf/hard of hearing and those with severe cognitive disabilities. These case studies are used to follow up the previous research with a more specific, in-depth look at how the media may impact specific groups of individuals.

Chapter Five

The Impact of the Media's Portrayal of Physical Disabilities

As he slowly pushes his way out of his wheelchair, Artie Abrams begins to explore his new-found ability and realize his one dream—he dances. After a dazzling display of footwork Artie crashes back to reality and his chair as he awakens from his daydream, "stuck" in his immobility (*Glee*, Season 1, Episode 19, "Dream On"). The rest of the episode explores the idea that Artie shares the same dream as all other individuals in wheelchairs, the desire to walk. While many critics praised the episode for further exploring the "disabled" character on the program (Doering 2009), there is a contradiction to an earlier episode in which the character has accepted and celebrates his disability. This contradictory imagery is not unique to *Glee* or other programs in which a character with a disability is highlighted within an episode or two. This may relate back to the supercrip imagery—look how well this character "deals" with their disability but also look what they have overcome (e.g., an inability to dance).

Physical representations of disability in the media, such as being in a wheelchair, are often depicted by individuals that do not have the disability in real life (or by cartoon characters, Bond 2008), enabling the characters to portray what life might be like without their disability, or, allowing characters to engage in behaviors that may not be typical, leaning again toward the supercrip representation of a disability. Producers have excused this with the need to be able to allow for flashbacks within storylines and the expenses that would be incurred for computer-generated imagery (Rosenburg 2013). This disability drag may have some significant implications on society and individuals with disabilities, particularly when it comes to the ability to identify with characters with disabilities.

IDENTIFICATION

The literature surrounding the media's depictions of disability shows that the media has the ability to draw an audience in and affect their lives through identification. Identifying with television characters is defined by Schramm, Lyle, and Parker (1961) as "the experience of being able to put oneself so deeply into a television character and feel oneself to be so like the character that one can feel the same emotions and experience the same events as the character is supposed to be feeling. This experience can contribute to personal identity formation" (as cited in McQuail 1994, 314). This process has also been linked to the sensation of taking on a character's identity and empathizing with individual characters (Moyer-Guse' 2008). The media has often been an important arena for basic information and social learning, including information that may be useful in identity formation. But the media also introduces people to phrases and images that are sometimes very effective conveyors of false information (Kitzinger, 1999) which viewers may not be aware of when consuming said messages. For some, media information can raise awareness of problems which had previously not been thought of as important. For example, if a media portrayal highlights a character being stigmatized for an inability to complete a task, a viewer may not have perceived the lack of task completion as important prior to said viewing. If this character is one in which a viewer previously identified, the effect may be problematic. (e.g., I identify with John, John can't climb a mountain, I have never thought about climbing a mountain, but I am now devastated that I will be unable to do so.) Miller and Philo (1999) posit that fictional media can produce very strong affective responses toward specific characters. Narrative formats such as what is found in fictional media, have been found to be more effective in providing information and changing attitudes, particularly when it comes to health information (Igartua and Casanova 2016).

Cohen (2001) defines character identification as a response through which viewers imagine themselves as being one of the characters of a program. This response generally occurs in instances where viewers find a television character to be realistic and they begin to find certain similarities between themselves and the character (Cohen 2001). Several studies have examined the importance of character identification on increasing the media's influence on viewers (Bandura 1986; Eyal and Rubin 2003; Zhou, Shapiro, and Wansink 2017). Identification is thought to increase the influence of media content due to the viewer's desire to be like or to behave like the character (Eyal and Rubin 2003). Kamins, Brand, Hoeke, and Moe (1989) argue that identification occurs when an individual adopts the behavior of another person because the individual aspires to be like that character. From this, we can see how identification with a television character would strengthen the influence of a character's expressed attitudes, beliefs, and/or behaviors on a viewer's own attitudes, beliefs, and/or behaviors. The viewer's desire to be like the character should facilitate agreement with or the adoption of some of the character's attributes.

The portrayal of disability in the media is concerning two fronts when it comes to identification: one, viewers identifying with characters and adopting their attitudes toward individuals with disabilities; two, viewers with a disability being able to identify with characters with disabilities. As noted above, if a viewer aspires to be like a character they have viewed on television, they are more likely to emulate their behaviors. When the media portrays disability, individuals that identify with certain characters may learn new ways of reacting toward disability, rather than someone merely preaching it to them (Hayakawa and Hayakawa 1993). Strong and Brown (2008) found positive results in this area when children that identified with a specific cartoon character reported a higher likelihood of modeling the character's positive treatment of people with disabilities. Going back to social cognitive theory, this would even strengthen the "reward" aspect as the viewer may be intrinsically rewarded for engaging in a behavior that makes them feel even more like the character they identify with on a program.

Even in Bond's (2008) study where portrayals were deemed to be more positive, the cartoon characters displaying disability were male, white and elderly, not necessarily the characters that children would identify with regardless of disability level. Also, characters with disabilities were minor characters (72%), who have less screen time and are less likely to be noticed than the main characters of a program. Further, chapter one points out the lack of characters with a disability in the media, in particular the lack of positively portrayed characters. So, the likelihood of finding and emulating identified characters' behavior, at this point in time, is not likely to be as fortunate as the Strong and Brown findings.

This lack of representation also impacts individuals with a disability and who is available to identify with within the media. If the only characters presented with a similar or the same disability are portrayed in a negative light, does identification occur? Will someone identify with a character simply because they share a disability? Additionally, if one cannot relate to a character with the same or similar disabilities in the media, there may be an impact on construction of one's personal identity (Kelly 2001). If I can't relate to a character with the same disability, will I begin to shift away from identifying with that disability at all? The media and identifying with characters help to construct the meaning of disability and societal attitudes. Engaging with media is a persistent social practice through which audiences carry out considerable rhetorical and cultural work within society (Kavoori 1999). If this work cannot be done between characters and individuals with disabilities, that limits the ability to construct one's own identity as well as having any impact on societal attitudes toward a disability.

As most do, individuals with disabilities develop identities within their own social contexts. This includes exposure to media presentation. Issues presented such as shame, stigma, or real/perceived barriers could impact the quality of life and well-being for individuals with disabilities (Turner and Szymanski 1990). This may be particularly relevant for individuals that develop a disability later in life. Smedema (2014) found that people will bring a "positive frame" to situations they encounter in life if they believe they are good enough and able to cope with life's challenges. Individuals will bring a "negative frame" to the same circumstances if they do not see themselves in such a favorable light. Zoller and Worrell (2006) found the media to have a direct impact on feelings of self-worth and that individuals with a disability could question their own perceptions of their identity based on the media's portrayal of a character. This can be particularly relevant for more visual/physical disabilities as viewers are more aware of the portrayal than with some of the more "hidden" disabilities. This concern also spreads to the larger viewing audience.

As chapters one and two presented the media's portrayal of disability, what do these findings mean for viewers? What do they mean for individuals with a physical disability? Findings have shown that the media's portrayal of disability is predominantly non-existent, negative, or questionably "too positive" (supercrip). As studies have shown that the media are a primary source of health information for the public, this may be particularly true for individuals who do not have direct experience with a disability (Sharf, Freimuth, Greenspon, and, Plotnick 1996). While those seeking out specific health information may utilize sources such as websites for information Walsh-Childers (2016) and Dutta-Bergman (2004) found that television is a primary source of health information for people that are not health oriented, so those individuals may not be conscious of their own or others' health issues. This would extend to individuals that do not have nor have thought about direct experience with an individuals with a disability. With the media as a primary source of information and if individuals believe that these portrayals are accurate, media theory and previous research show that false representations have the ability to negatively impact not only viewers but real people with a disability.

Studies have found negative and potentially damaging effects of the media's portrayal of disability and its influence on people viewing these portrayals (Farnall and Smith 1999, Renwick 2016) and those who have a disability (Zoller and Worrell 2006). Further, findings show that negative portrayals do little to reduce currently held negative perceptions of disabilities within the public and may reinforce stereotypes (Foss 2014b). Farnall and Smith (1999) found that viewers of positive portrayals of characters with disabilities had reduced feelings of anger, fear, or concern regarding encounters with individuals with disabilities. However, even the positive portrayals of disability did not reduce discomfort at the thought of interacting with such individuals. It should be noted, however, that representations of the supercrip were more predominant with physical disabilities than cognitive disabilities.

To add to the examination, and outside of broader findings presented in chapter 1, a few studies have remained specific to physical disabilities. Ganahl and Arbuckle (2001), looking specifically at physical disabilities within the media, found these roles to be "virtually nonexistent," so it makes sense that there is little research in the area of portrayals as well. The few studies that did examine the portrayal of physical disability on its own within the media were not found to be predominantly positive in representation. For example, Ellis (2003) not only discusses the anger of those with physical disabilities expressed in the media due to an "inability to accept their own limitations" (114) but also the idea that death may be the most merciful outcome (an example of the previously discussed "one who shouldn't have survived" from Nelson [2000]). A less recent study, Longmore (1987), also found that suicide was seen as a release within the media for characters with a physical disability as they can then escape their "catastrophic disablement." Both of these portrayals highlight the most extreme negative aspects of individuals with physical disabilities—the "otherness" that exists between those with and without physical disabilities and the hopelessness of individuals that cannot perform as "normal" members of society. Taken to the extreme, these acts that are almost sacrificial in that one should rather die than live with a physical disability.

MEDIA REPRESENTATIONS OF PHYSICAL DISABILITY IMPACT ON SOCIETY

In general, findings of previous research show that the portrayal of physical disability has both negative and positive effects on society. First and foremost, studies reinforced the idea that physical disabilities are underrepresented in the media. Much of the theoretical discussion of the impact of the media relies on a lack of direct experience. That negative assumptions regarding physical disability are "acquired through the 'normal' learning process" (Barnes 1991, 46). And, much like racist or sexist attitudes, may be so much a part of our culture due to duplications in the media. Barnes further found that the absence of physical disability from the media tied to portrayed links between individuals with physical disability and medicine reinforce the idea that individuals with disabilities are ill and not able to fully participate in life.

Longmore (1987) points out society's tendency to shun and stigmatize what we fear. The anxiety of physical disability happening to an "able-bodied" person is eased when we see disability presented as "punishment for evil"; that people with disabilities are disillusioned by their fate, and that those individuals with disabilities resent those without and in fact would "destroy them" (Longmore 1987, 134). Marilyn Dahl's (1993) study, "The Role of the Media in Promoting Images of Disability—Disability as Metaphor: The Evil Crip" posits that the convention has been to present physical deformity or any visible defect within the frame of "symbolizing evil." In a more recent study, Donnelly (2016) examines the negative archetypes of disability in fantasy and the role that society plays in labelling and ostracizing the "others" in the media. By keeping up the stigmatization of physical disability through villainous characters, the non-disabled viewers are reassured (after all Captain Hook was a bad guy and deserved to lose a hand, right?) that physical disability is simply an "emblem of evil."

Several studies have focused specifically on how the representation of individuals with a physical disability might impact society. For example, Cole and associates (2003) found that negative portrayals increased prejudice toward individuals with a physical disability. Adults of all abilities found "pitiful" portrayals (victims or those needing exorbitant care) led to more negative views of disability. These negative portrayals, when causing discomfort or confirming stereotypes, can reinforce and strengthen society's negative attitudes (Donaldson 1981). Looking at some specific characters, Elliott and Byrd (1983) examined blindness through a character on the television show *Mork & Mindy*. They found that there was no increase in tolerance toward individuals that are blind after viewing the portrayal. However, subjects exposed to an educational film about individuals that were blind did show a short-term attitude change. As has been repeatedly expressed, previous findings show a limited and decidedly negative portrayal of physical disability in the media, so negative effects on society would not be surprising. What about when the portrayals examined for impact are positive?

As noted, some individuals praise networks simply for airing an episode containing a character with a disability, whereas many researchers would prefer to see positive portrayals in hopes that the congruity principle will take place. Byrd (1989) highlights the congruity principle from Osgood and Tannenbaum (1955), which looks at someone with a preconceived negative attitude for a disability. If they like or have a positive attitude about a television character with the same disability, their attitude for both will shift to a more neutral place. For example, if I have a firm negative belief that people in wheelchairs are not productive members of society, I may have a negative attitude toward people in wheelchairs. However, if I am a fan of Dr. Robbins on *CSI*, who is in a wheelchair, my attitude about individuals in wheelchairs may shift to a more neutral area (not a complete 180 but less negative). Thus, if one has a negative attitude and dislikes a character or has a positive attitude then likes a character, these attitudes will be reinforced and strengthened. Most research into the impact of representations is more survey based versus experimental; therefore, it is difficult to truly ascertain any attitude change when viewing negative or positive portrayals. But, if one follows the congruity principle, positive portrayals within the media should either reinforce previous positive beliefs or shift those with negative beliefs to a more neutral or positive attitude, possibly reducing stigmatization or marginalization.

Several studies found limited impact from positive portrayals to positive attitudes. Nancy Glauberman (1980) in an experiment found that after children viewed a positive portrayal of physical disability on television (an episode of *Sesame Street* with a character in a wheelchair), there were improved attitudes and behavioral intentions of children toward their peers with physical disabilities. Farnall and Smith (1999), after surveying adults regarding their viewing of certain programs with characters with disabilities, also found that positive portrayals could lead to decreases in perceptions of negative attributes of individuals with a disability. However, even when effects research found that positive portrayals were related to positive attitudes, respondents were still reporting low levels of comfort (Farnall and Smith 1999), that mental health services in residential neighborhoods might endanger residents (Diefenbach and West 2007), and some children, even after viewing a positive portrayal, still didn't understand the disability (Diamond and Kensinger 2002). It is important to note, regarding children and the impact of the media on their attitudes and behaviors regarding disability, that research shows that the understanding of disability is complex; however, an easy source for information on health issues is television.

Further analysis points to a lack of success with positive portrayals of physical disability in the media on society. Farnall and Smith (1999) found that after viewing *Rainman* respondents still said they were uncomfortable with individuals that were blind, in a wheelchair and physically disfigured (i.e., seeing a positive representation of any disability may not carry across to other disabilities). Mares and Acosta (2008) had children viewing a prosocial message regarding a character playing with a three-legged dog. They found that children didn't really "get" the message of inclusion and that they had an increased concern for germs (the dog lost its leg due to germs) rather than an increase in tolerance for those with physical disabilities. While the impact on overall media consumers is important since the media plays a role in shaping societal knowledge and understanding of physical disability, it is also important to understand the media's impact on those with a physical disability.

Quinlan and Bates (2008) found that individuals reporting on and blogging about Heather Mills, a celebrity with a partial leg amputation that appeared on *Dancing with the Stars*, were mixed regarding the potential impact on society. Whereas her presentation was commonly framed with a supercrip narrative—she is dancing—she is complete, some struggled with the juxtaposition, saying she can't be a dancer and "sick" at the same time. Further, some felt that Mills is taking advantage of the sick role for sympathy or special treatment. For people with physical disabilities the presentation was seen as "not fair" as she can afford the right prostheses for dancing and her amputation was below the knee versus at her hip, allowing for uncommon mobility on her prosthesis. This leads to an important discussion of media representation—how are these portrayals impacting individuals with disabilities?

MEDIA REPRESENTATIONS OF PHYSICAL DISABILITY IMPACT ON INDIVIDUALS WITH A PHYSICAL DISABILITY

Research into the effects of media representation of physical disability on individuals with a physical disability has been very limited. [1] However, much like the impact on society, positive, negative, and mixed outcomes have been found. While Ross (1997) found that her sample of adults with disabilities were very critical of portrayals in the media as stereotypical and unrealistic, that even supercrip presentations were hard to relate to (as did Quinlan and Bates 2008 findings), two studies, Zhang and Haller (2013) and Kama (2004) found that their sample appreciated the positive portrayals of supercrips. Zhang and Haller had the most positively affected group with most reporting on the impact of supercrips as increasing their own positive attitudes toward being disabled. On the other hand, Kama found diverse results with his sample population split on their reactions. Some looked to the supercrips as role models while others criticized, charging that the portrayal was damaging to their self-respect, particularly if they could not achieve the same levels of success as the character.

When further examining the impact of negative portrayals on individuals with a disability, the findings have been consistent in regard to the negative impact taking place. Ross (1997), in her two reception studies, looked across a wide range of individuals with disabilities. She found that there was widespread sadness and irritation regarding the stereotypical portrayal often found in the media. When it comes to physical disability the wheelchair has become an "emblem of disability" that is frequently used simply to add or signal a disability within a program. This, of course, might cause individuals with other physical impairments to wonder if their disability is too unacceptable for mainstream television.

Amit Kama (2004) conducted interviews with individuals with physical disabilities, focusing on two themes based on his results—the supercrip and the "pitiful handicapped." The representation of pitiful handicapped in the media directly impacted Kama's interviewees by making them feel ostracized, weak, and ashamed. Individuals with disabilities felt very disconnected as the presentation in the media was very different from their own perceived identities. However, the participants did imply that the impact of such representation may be more damaging on how others treat them than on their own identity. Therefore, to combat the stereotypes and possible exclusion, some respondents reported preferring an unrealistic supercrip portrayal. While recognizing the potential backfiring of being unable to fulfill others' expectations based on these portrayals, many respondents preferred such a "beacon of hope, a model for admiration and emulation" (462).

There is much discussion in disability studies regarding the supercrip portrayal and the impact on individuals with physical disabilities, particularly as the aforementioned results of such portrayals are very mixed. In this area, the differences between individuals with same or similar disabilities is highlighted. In a program a character may be in a wheelchair due to an accident, injury, as the symptom of an illness, or a variety of other reasons. Some may have mobility from the waist up and others may have little to no movement from the neck down. Everyone is different. For some, the supercrip portrayal may be completely unattainable and they may be affected by the media's portrayal of someone with a similar physical impairment. For example, in the study conducted by Heather Zoller and myself in 2006, some participants were unable to reconcile with a character that had the same illness yet was able to perform physical tasks that they were unable to do (but others didn't have the same reaction as they were able to perform such tasks). Further, others questioned why they were physically unable to perform some of the tasks that someone in the media was able to do with the same illness. Again, those with similar physical limitations as the character did not feel the same disconnect or negative reactions from others as those that had the same disability yet different limitations.

Ultimately, as representation has remained low and portrayals have remained negative, the effects on individuals with disabilities have remained mixed, with negative or stereotypical portrayals doing little to increase positive perceptions of individuals with disabilities. It is, unsurprisingly, only those few positive portrayals that seem to have a positive impact on overall viewers. But, those have even been found to have negative effects on individuals with the portrayed disability (Zoller and Worrell 2006) as well. Social identity theory highlights the use of comparison in managing identity and particularly the role that the media can play in this process (Hardwood 1999). Following this idea, if individuals are continuously comparing themselves to characters within the media, yet there are few, if any, characters similar to themselves, how might this influence their perceptions of self? This may be highlighted by whether the few portrayals are perceived as positive or negative as well. But, can this all be rectified by a program that contains several characters with the same sensory impairment and that has mostly been seen as a positive representation of a disability? While little primary research exists within this area, the following case study examines a specific portrayal of deaf/hard of hearing individuals within the media and its impact.

NOTE

1. Several researchers theorize about the impact after presenting the representation of physical disability in the media, and common sense alone would say that seeing a presentation of someone with a physical disability killing themselves because their physical disability makes them "unworthy" (Ellis 2003) would have a significant impact on individuals with a physical disability.

Chapter Six

A Case Study of the Media's Impact on Individuals That Are Deaf/Hard of Hearing

In 2013, the television program *Switched at Birth* aired an entire episode ("Uprising") from the "deaf perspective." Most of the episode was in silence with a few spoken words at the beginning and end, to give audience members a feel for what individuals who are deaf/hard of hearing go through on a daily basis (while silent, the program still uses American Sign Language communication throughout the episode). Cast members, including Oscar winner Marlee Matlin, called the episode "a risk" and "history making" and were excited for hearing audience members to have this experience (CTV News 2013). Making history is not new for the program as *Switched at Birth's* main characters are two teen girls, one of which is deaf, and the program incorporates ASL and Deaf culture in every episode. The program has predominantly been praised in mainstream media for its groundbreaking use of sign language, the "respectful depiction" of individuals that are deaf/hard of hearing and as a "voice for those with hearing loss (Bamey 2012; Hayer 2011; Starr 2017). But others have reported discontent with the program for its "late to deafness" main actress, ASL fluency of some of the characters, use of simultaneous communication, and its hearing perspective of Deaf culture (the show is written and directed by hearing individuals) (Redeafined 2013).

Switched at Birth debuted on June 6, 2011, running for five seasons on ABC Family. The program follows two families that discover their daughters were switched at birth. Bay Kennish, a teenager from a wealthy suburb of Kansas, is actually the biological daughter of Regina Vasquez, a single mother living in a much less affluent neighborhood. Daphne Vasquez, also a teenager, was born to John and Kathryn Kennish but raised by Regina. Daphne lost her hearing at the age of three. Plotlines and story arcs center around the two families trying to deal with the news of the switch as well as the world of the Deaf community. Each episode incorporates ASL and subtitles and characters that are hard of hearing or deaf played mostly by actors that are deaf/hard of hearing. Katie LeClerc, Daphne, while not deaf in real life is hard of hearing as a symptom of her Meniere's disease.

Perhaps the most famous cast member on the program is Marlee Matlin. Matlin, who has been deaf since she was 18 months old, has been acting since the age of seven and won an Oscar for her 1986 performance in *Children of a Lesser God*. With her long career, Matlin has usually been the only actor or character that is deaf/hard of hearing on a program. Says Matlin of this unique program, "I thought, all these years of doing television and I've never seen such a phenomenal reception from having a deaf character in a show, not just telling stories about deaf victims but actually deaf story lines looking at the culture and the language. It's a fascinating aspect you've never seen on television before, combined with good writing and good acting. It's just something I'm really proud to be a part of" (Owen 2013, B1). (This show also highlights some areas of interest from section one; it is a show that has several members with similar levels of deafness/hard of hearing, is discussed as a positive portrayal by viewers as well as in the media, and within the popular press discussion, individuals from the program are being interviewed by popular press outlets for their viewpoints.)

While the program is raising awareness of deafness, it is important to examine these fictional representations. The accuracy of such portrayals is examined in connection to the perceived impact on individuals that are deaf/hard of hearing—their identity, perception of self and perceived societal impact. The examination of characters that are deaf/hard of hearing was chosen for this analysis of the media for three reasons: 1. As mentioned, *Switched at Birth* is one of the first fictional programs on television centered around characters with a sensory impairment of deaf/hard of hearing and not just highlighting a few characters in one or two episodes. Therefore, viewers are presented a very rich exposure to a specific group of portrayals.[1] 2. Even for those that argue that deaf/hard of hearing is not a disability, individuals that are deaf/hard of hearing are a part of a large minority group with a sensory limitation. 3. The program focuses more specifically and explicitly on individuals that are deaf/hard of hearing (unlike programs that may bring in a character in a wheelchair for unknown reasons or someone with an unidentified, "hidden" disability).

DEAF/HARD OF HEARING AND DISABILITY

Prior to an in-depth discussion regarding deaf/hard of hearing and the media, it is first important to discuss Deaf, deaf, and hard of hearing in the context of disability. Like many other individuals facing physical limitations, many within the Deaf community would not appreciate the label of having a disability. As the aforementioned World Health Organization definition of disability used for this text includes all impairments, activity limitations, and participation restrictions, a wide net is cast which does include sensory impairments such as hard of hearing/deafness, hence why it is included in this text and is used for this case study. This case study does not delve into the intricacies of Deaf culture to greatly further this conversation or argue for labeling anyone as disabled, but two resources are recommended for consideration. Susan Burch and Ian Sutherland (2006) in their article, "Who's Not Here Yet? American Disability History," give an in-depth reflection on disabilities and minorities within a historical context. Within the essay, they present a compelling history and discussion of deafness and the label of disability. Of particular interest is the discussion regarding the rejection of the term disability within the Deaf community.

Also, it is important to recognize that scholars within Deaf studies have pointed out that simply using the term "disability" already marginalizes individuals and contributes to audism within society as discussed in H-Dirksen L. Bauman's (2004) article, "Audism: Exploring the Metaphysics of Oppression." Audism is discrimination against individuals based on hearing ability and that those that can hear are somehow superior to those that cannot. This concern of labeling leading to stigmatization is not limited to the Deaf community. Previous research has examined instances of marginalization with illnesses such as cancer (Bresnahan, Silk, and Zhuang 2009), physical disfigurement (Park, Faulkner, and Schaller 2003) and visual impairment (Ryan, Bajorek, Beaman, and Anas 2005), to name a few.

According to the National Center for Health Statistics, 15% of adults over the age of 18 have reported some trouble hearing (Blackwell, Lucas, Clarke 2014). Despite the almost 38 million people that have trouble hearing, there is still a great lack of information regarding deafness and hearing loss. One area that is particularly overlooked is Deaf culture. According to Padden and Humphries (2005) in their book *Inside Deaf Culture* the capitalized "Deaf" is used to denote the culture surrounding the beliefs and practices of a community that uses sign language in everyday life. The lowercase "deaf" refers to lack of function of the ears' ability to hear. The cultural entrenchment by individuals that are deaf/hard of hearing may play a role in how an individual identifies within society.

IDENTITY AND INDIVIDUALS THAT ARE DEAF/HARD OF HEARING

Chapter 3 of this text discusses identity and sense of self. The deaf/hard of hearing identity is vastly different from most physical disabilities. The Deaf community has a distinct, cohesive subculture with its own norms and values, not to mention its own common language, Sign Language (Ladd 2003). As Carter and Mireles (2016a) point out the uniqueness of the Deaf community and identity within, a part of that is the positive/negative duality presented. If one is embraced by the Deaf community, then they are likely negatively stigmatized within society. Further, their study on deaf identity and depression speaks to the Deaf identity as one that "provides meaning and purpose in life" (510).

As mentioned, the Deaf, deaf, hard of hearing communities can be very unique. For example, individuals that are more committed to being active members of the Deaf community are likely to identify more strongly within the Deaf identity. Individuals that are deaf/hard of hearing but are not as entrenched in the cultural aspects of the Deaf community may feel their identities shaped by other aspects of their lives. According to Bat-Chava (2000) some individuals will eschew the Deaf identity and assimilate as much as possible into the hearing world, assuming a "culturally hearing identity." Carter and Mireles (2016a) provide the example of "if a deaf individual has a highly prominent Deaf identity, it means that being a deaf person is crucial to who they are and that they feel it is highly important to be a deaf person. Identity prominence varies depending on how often one gets support from others for an identity, how committed one is to the identity, and the amount of rewards one receives that are associated with the identity" (516).

Further research into the Deaf identity focuses on shared experiences and social construction. For some individuals that are deaf/hard of hearing, the ability to share negative experiences within their community aids in reducing negative self-concepts and vice versa with positive in-group experiences. There is also the role that family and social support may play; findings have shown differences in identity shaping based on something as simple as whether an individual that is deaf/hard of hearing is born to parents that are deaf/hard of hearing or whether their family learns sign language to communicate or not (Bat-Chava 2000). Other aspects of society may also play a role in the understanding and shaping of identity, such as the media.

PORTRAYAL OF CHARACTERS THAT ARE DEAF/HARD OF HEARING IN THE MEDIA

Foss (2014b) in her analysis of identity in television's representations of d/ Deafness points out that most of the characters that are deaf/hard of hearing are limited to guest status, such as a seldom seen friend or date of a main character within a program. She further examines presentation under two models—pathological and cultural. The pathological model is much like the traditional model presented in chapter 2. Individuals that are deaf/hard of hearing are dependent on "cures" such as cochlear implants to be "normal" and they are dependent on others to survive within society. The cultural model is more reflective of the progressive model where characters are independent and their deafness is just one of their many qualities/traits. Golos (2010) also uses the pathological and cultural models in her examination of characters that are deaf in children's television programs. She found that most of the language used in programs with characters that are deaf/hard of hearing followed the pathological model with frequent references to the characters "inabilities" and the emphasis that individuals that are deaf/hard of hearing can and implicitly should fit themselves into the hearing world. There were some positive cultural representations in her analysis as well, such as acknowledging American Sign Language as a language versus simply stating that a character is using hand movements to communicate.

Further studies have found similar results regarding the portrayal of characters that are deaf/hard of hearing in the media. The media presents characters as needing to be treated (Foss 2009), as "wild savages" (Foss 2014b), and as exotic "others" (Kincheloe 2010), again highlighting the us versus them between individuals that are hearing and those that are deaf/hard of hearing. Much of the presentation of characters within the media has been found to reinforce real world stigmas of deafness since many individuals receive their information about Deaf culture or deafness through media representations (Haller 2010).

As has been discussed, studies have shown that television programs have been effective in influencing viewers on a number of attributes. However, much of the media information provided has been inaccurate, misleading, and/or leads to stigmatization of individuals with physical disabilities. One aspect that is challenging is when there are few or only negative representations for examination. If characters that are deaf/hard of hearing are relegated to the "outside" on television, then their impact may be on increasing feelings of otherness within those that are deaf/hard of hearing. However, when a program centers on characters that are deaf/hard of hearing, new avenues for identification are opened to individuals that have been traditionally marginalized by society. As Golos (2010) points out, little is known about possible impacts from a program that highlights the inclusion and culture of a minority group. This research takes a specific look into the impact of the media (and particularly the program *Switched at Birth*) on individuals that are deaf/hard of hearing and their perceptions of the impact these portrayals have on their identity as well as how society may view those that are deaf/hard of hearing.

I felt that it was important to conduct primary research to help us better examine the impact of media representation. Aside from the lack of current research that exists in this area, having something unique to examine should give better understanding and insight into these possible effects. Therefore, the following research questions are posed and examined: How do individuals that are deaf/hard of hearing perceive the portrayal of characters that are deaf/hard of hearing on *Switched at Birth*? Which characters are people identifying with within in the program *Switched at Birth*? How have portrayals of *Switched at Birth* characters that are deaf/hard of hearing impacted the identity of individuals that are deaf/hard of hearing? What is the perceived societal impact of portrayals of *Switched at Birth* characters that are deaf/hard of hearing?

METHODS

Procedure

As the focus of this study was to examine the impact of a specific program on individuals that were deaf/hard of hearing, several methods were undertaken to gather the sample. I am extremely fortunate to have had access to individuals at a large northeastern university with a significantly large population of deaf and hard of hearing students. A number of individuals were recruited to share a survey with students. Snowball sampling was also used to have deaf and hard of hearing students forward the survey to others outside of the university to attempt to widen the demographics of the sample. While the program *Switched at Birth* predominantly targets individuals 18–24, it is important to gather data from individuals of various ages and education levels.

Once individuals were recruited, they were given a link to an online survey. Participants were asked to fill out the survey, which included questions regarding representations of individuals that are deaf/hard of hearing within the media, specifically on the program *Switched at Birth*, as well as questions regarding the perceived impact of such portrayals. It should be noted that the survey was presented in the traditional text format, whereas a preferred format for some individuals that are deaf/hard of hearing may be the video signing format. However, as the majority of participants were college students and acclimated to this style of presentation, it was deemed acceptable.

Measures

The survey began with items regarding the representation of disability within television programs. Using a 5-point Likert scale with 1 = Strongly Disagree and 5 = Strongly Agree, items looked at overall visibility of disability, such as, "Individuals with physical disabilities are visible on television programs." Then items moved to focus on characters that are deaf/hard of hearing: "Characters that are deaf/hard of hearing are visible on television programs." There were 12 items pertaining to overall accuracy and representation of characters that are deaf/hard of hearing such as, "I believe that people that are deaf/hard of hearing are like those that are on television." After the more general items, the survey focused on the representation on *Switched at Birth*. Participants were asked if they had viewed the program; if not, they were taken to some general questions and then ended with basic demographics. If they responded that they had seen the program, they were taken to specific questions regarding the program and representation of deaf/hard of hearing characters on the show.

Participants were asked about their perceptions of the role of deafness within the program. The first three items focused on the visibility of characters that are deaf/hard of hearing. Using a 5-point Likert scale with 1 = Strongly Disagree and 5 = Strongly Agree, respondents were asked items such as, "are characters that are deaf/hard of hearing are frequently seen on *Switched at Birth*." Additionally, three items looked at the accuracy of the portrayal such as, "I believe that characters on *Switched at Birth* that are deaf/hard of hearing accurately show what it is like to be deaf or hard of hearing." The final nine items here focused on specific characteristics or attributes of characters such as, "The characters that are deaf/hard of hearing on *Switched at Birth* are portrayed as less capable than hearing characters" and comparisons to hearing characters such as, "The characters that are deaf/hard of hearing on *Switched at Birth* are portrayed as easier to get along with than hearing characters."

Survey respondents were then asked questions regarding characters that they may identify with, both hearing and deaf/hard of hearing. Respondents were first asked which hearing character reminded them most of themselves. Then they were asked six items using a 5-point Likert scale, with 1 = Strongly Disagree and 5 = Strongly Agree, to examine if respondents believed characters were "similar to me" or if they "identify with this character." These items were followed by seven items using a Semantic-Differential scale asking about things such as behavior, similarity, social class, and culture. These items were repeated for deaf/hard of hearing characters so respondents answered the same items, thinking of one hearing character and then again thinking of a character that is deaf/hard of hearing.

Following these questions, items specific to identity and perceived societal impact were asked. Close-ended Likert items (1 = Strongly Disagree; 5 = Strongly Agree) were asked regarding how participants believed the characters on *Switched at Birth* impacted their identity, how they feel about themselves, and how they perceive the show may have an impact on how others treat them. These were each followed by an open-ended question to better explain these beliefs. Finally, the survey ends with questions regarding hearing status and other demographic questions.

FINDINGS

A total of 43 individuals participated in the case study. Of these participants, 20 identified as deaf or hard of hearing. The participants were mostly Caucasian (67%) with a relatively even distribution of males and females. The average age of participants was 33 years old. Almost half of the participants had seen *Switched at Birth* (49%) at some time.

Prior to answering the research questions focusing on *Switched at Birth*, we can look at the overall perceived representation of physical disability and deaf/hard of hearing within the media. Participants were relatively neutral (M = 3.24, SD = 1.06) regarding the visibility of physical disability within the media. There was no difference amongst participants that were deaf/hard of hearing and hearing individuals regarding the perception. However, participants did disagree with the visibility of deaf/hard of hearing characters on television (M = 2.84, SD = 1.19). When asked about frequency of visibility of deaf/hard of hearing characters, the numbers continue to decrease (M = 2.14, SD = 1.04), with hearing participants (M = 2.37, SD = 1.17) reporting slightly more frequency than deaf/hard of hearing participants (M = 1.95, SD = .95). When examining overall positivity of the portrayal (the 9 item scale) one item did not properly load to the scale and was subsequently dropped from examination. The remaining portrayal scale (α = .70) found that the group had an overall neutral (M = 3.33, SD = .68) feeling about the overall portrayal of individuals that are deaf/hard of hearing in the media.

Research question one asked about the perceived portrayal of characters that are deaf/hard of hearing on *Switched at Birth*. Overall, the portrayal was perceived as visible (M = 4.16, SD = 1.02) and slightly accurate (M = 3.32, SD = 1.16), with individuals reporting that characters presented a slightly positive representation of what it is like to be deaf/hard of hearing (M = 3.42, SD = .96). Individuals that are deaf/hard of hearing found the *Switched at Birth* characters to be slightly more visible (M = 4.22, SD = 1.09) than those of hearing viewers (M = 4.00, SD = 1.00). Individuals that are deaf/hard of hearing also found that deaf/hard of hearing characters were seen with more frequency (M = 4.00, SD = 1.22) than hearing participants' perceptions (M =

3.89, SD = 1.27). When it comes to accuracy of the portrayals of deaf/hard of hearing individuals, respondents that were deaf/hard of hearing believed the portrayals to be more accurate (M = 3.56, SD = 1.13) than hearing participants (M = 2.89, SD = 1.05). When examining portrayals, again one item was dropped from the 9 item scale, creating a scale examining the portrayal of individuals that are deaf/hard of hearing on *Switched at Birth* (α = .73). Once again, respondents believed the portrayal to be relatively neutral (M = 3.29, SD = .73).

Research question two focused on who individuals were identifying with on the program. Of the hearing characters, most participants identified with Bay Kennish (37%) the teenage girl that was "switched," and Regina Vasquez (16%). The strength of identifying with these characters utilizing the 5 item identification scale (α = .78) found no difference between the respondents that were hearing (M = 3.26, SD = .46) and deaf/hard of hearing (M = 3.48, SD = .61).

For the characters that are deaf/hard of hearing, the majority of respondents identified with teens Daphne Vasquez (58%), the other half of the "switch," and Emmett Bledsoe (21%). The strength of identifying with these characters was higher because both hearing (M = 4.41, SD = .89) and participants that were deaf/hard of hearing (M = 5.22, SD = 1.05) had a higher (though not quite significantly so) identification with the characters chosen.

The third research question asks if the portrayals of *Switched at Birth* characters that are deaf/hard of hearing impacted the identity of individuals that are deaf/hard of hearing. Both close- and open-ended questions were used to examine this question. Items examined overall characters that are deaf/hard of hearing and then the specific characters on *Switched at Birth*. Findings were relatively neutral when it comes to the overall impact of characters that are deaf/hard of hearing on how participants felt about themselves (M = 3.89, SD = .78) on their identity (M = 3.33, SD = 1.32). Interestingly, these numbers significantly increased when examining the characters on *Switched at Birth* with an impact on feelings about themselves (M = 5.44, SD = 1.51) t (8) = 5.29, p = .001 and with the impact on identity (M = 4.11, SD = 2.03) t (8) = 2.80, p = .023.

Additionally, open-ended questions found respondents feeling that the media's overall portrayal of characters that are deaf/hard of hearing impacts how they feel about themselves both positively and negatively. From the general, "I believe the portrayal of deaf/hard of hearing in the media is not well represented, and has a negative impact on people how to act with me [sic]" or "There really isn't much of a portrayal, so it kind of sucks not getting to see any representation of something I deal with 24/7 in basically any media" to more specific "I think it has helped me reflect on how I am similar or different to them in social situations and in my life in general. I rarely get a chance to do that otherwise." When speaking of identity, some spoke of not comparing themselves to others and that their identities were already formed prior to ever seeing a fictional character that was deaf/hard of hearing or just not really knowing if there was any impact, "I don't think it has but I'm not sure. Maybe on some unconscious level." Others had both positive and negative thoughts on the impact on identity. For example, one respondent reported that seeing individuals who are deaf/hard of hearing in the media has "strengthened my identity within the deaf community and has made me more confident with my identity overall," whereas another respondent reports that "it's just not that relative to me," showing a lack of identification with characters that are deaf/hard of hearing.

The final research question looks at the perceived societal impact of the portrayals of deaf/hard of hearing on *Switched at Birth*. For this, respondents focused on how they believed the portrayal might impact their treatment by others. When asked about the overall portrayals of characters that are deaf/hard of hearing, respondents felt that they did slightly impact how others treated them ($M = 3.67$, $SD = .87$) whereas, when asked to focus on *Switched at Birth*, respondents felt this portrayal had a significantly higher impact on how others treat them ($M = 4.56$, $SD = 1.67$), $t(8) = 2.29$, $p = .05$.

DISCUSSION

This case study is simply a glimpse into the current possibilities surrounding the portrayal of individuals that are deaf/hard of hearing in the media. This is a unique examination as the focus is on a portrayal that has predominantly been found to be positive and examines individuals with many similarities to several of the characters of the program. First, there were several previous findings supported with this research. The overall visibility of all physical disabilities was deemed relatively neutral (individuals neither agreed nor disagreed that individuals with physical disabilities were seen in the media). However, when focusing on characters that were deaf/hard of hearing, participants did not believe that there was high visibility or frequency of such characters. These two findings are very similar to previous research examining the number of individuals with a physical disability in the media and when examining both physical disability (e.g. from the early work of Head [1954] to the more recent Bond [2008] or Worrell [2012]) and specifically characters that are deaf/hard of hearing (Foss 2014b). Individuals that reported as deaf/hard of hearing disagreed even more strongly than those that were hearing, regarding the frequency of individuals portrayed. One area that is slightly different from early research but more in line with some current findings is in the positivity of the portrayal of individuals that are deaf/hard of hearing in the media. Participants found the representation to be relatively neutral, neither positive or negative across media. So, while critics glowingly report on the positivity of the portrayal on *Switched at Birth*, viewers that are deaf/hard of hearing find it to be slightly above neutral. This finding lends some question to the examination of so-called positive portrayals in the media designated by those without the characteristics in question.

Interestingly, the portrayal of Deaf community and culture was not perceived as very accurate by hearing viewers (as it was by those that are deaf/hard of hearing). Following the elaboration likelihood model, it may be that those that are deaf/hard of hearing are paying more attention to the information provided and therefore analyzing it more thoroughly, whereas those that are using the peripheral route are simply responding to what usually occurs within the media—inaccurate presentation. Or, does the show not fit into preconceived stereotypes held by individuals that are hearing? Perhaps there is even more to be discovered regarding screen size of viewing. While additional questions were not asked in this area, it would be interesting to know why there is discrepancy here.

When it comes to examining how media portrayals might impact individuals that are deaf/hard of hearing and how they feel about themselves as well as their identity, there were significant increases in both when examining overall media portrayals versus the more specific program. As expected, there was not strong identification with the hearing characters by individuals that are deaf/hard of hearing. However, this increased drastically with the identification with characters that were deaf. Within the same program, and having characters of similar age, Bay and Daphne, the deaf/hard of hearing character saw an increase in identification. While the open-ended responses were mixed regarding how individuals that are deaf/hard of hearing feel about themselves based on the portrayal, it is clear that participants felt some level of impact.

Much like feelings of self-perception, feelings about the perceived societal impact of the portrayals of deaf/hard of hearing significantly increased when focusing on a program that portrays characters that are deaf/hard of hearing versus the overall media landscape presentation. It may be that in research regarding the impact of disability, a general overview (e.g., simply examining "physical disability") will find less impactful results than focusing on specific characters such as within this case study.

As mentioned in examining the media's impact on identity, individuals that are less certain about themselves and their belonging within a group may be more likely to allow the media to play a role in shaping identity. Participants in this case study were not asked about their levels of identifying within the Deaf community. Those that are more fully engrained in the Deaf culture may have already been comfortable and set in their identity prior to viewing the program, whereas others new to the Deaf community or less involved may see a stronger impact on their identity. Of course, this is only a case study of information to examine a specific program and not meant to be generalizable to the entire population of individuals that are deaf/hard of hearing. Further examination into the impact of representations of cognitive disabilities are in the following chapters.

NOTE

1. As the next section discusses, it is not my intention to debate the term "disability" in relation to individuals that are deaf/hard of hearing. As, at this time, *Switched at Birth* is the only fictional program that has not only revolved around a single character that is deaf/hard of hearing but multiple characters with varying degrees of deafness, we are presented with a unique opportunity when it comes to presentation, character identification, and impact of the program. I am utilizing the WHO definition of disability to clarify and reduce any offense that may be had.

Chapter Seven

The Impact of the Media's Portrayal of Cognitive Disabilities

Suffering from his inability to get past his many phobias and obsessive-compulsive disorder, Adrian Monk consents to a new medication. The morning after he takes a pill, lo and behold a whole new detective emerges. Miraculously cured, Monk begins to display a social style and lack of care counter to the man beloved by his friends. He stops caring about anyone or anything and generally becomes apathetic. He has also lost his ability to do his job, solve cases, and be a "modern day Sherlock Holmes." Apparently, all of his power lies in his disability. By the end of the episode Monk's assistant has tossed his pills and the audience is assured that the eccentric detective is back ("Mr. Monk Takes His Medicine" Season 3, *Monk*). Much like the Artie example in chapter 4, Adrian Monk seems to want to be cured of his disability. When that changes him too drastically and he realizes that being "normal" is not for him, he simply throws away the medication that has changed everything about him. The magic of television and disability drag; one-minute OCD and phobic, the next cured, then back again.

Unlike Artie, and other characters with physical disabilities, one can't "see" Monk's disability. With cognitive disabilities, the viewer isn't able to see how the brain is processing information and exactly how someone is cognitively disabled. Similar to physical disabilities, individuals portraying characters with cognitive disabilities usually do not have that disability in real life (that we know of). One of the most current exceptions to this is when characters have Down syndrome. (In fact, in what I have discovered thus far, Down syndrome may be just about the only cognitive disability that does not suffer from disability drag within fictional media.) So, much like Artie and Adrian, producers can have their actors engage in onscreen scenarios of "normalcy," whether that be through dream sequences or miraculous medication. While physical disabilities show more reliance on others for task-oriented behaviors (e.g., gaining access to buildings), cognitive disabilities can be more implicit and difficult to accurately portray in the media. This all leads to interest in the social construction of disability.

SOCIAL CONSTRUCTION OF DISABILITY

The impact that these media portrayals are likely to have on beliefs and attitudes (particularly for those viewers with no direct experience with individuals with said disability) may play a role in the social construction of that disability. This in turn could affect the disabled individual's role in their social community and how they are treated. Let's take an example from this text, our psychotic friend Floyd Feylinn Ferrell. Ferrell is institutionalized for an abstract cognitive disability of "mental illness" (after taking a bite out of his younger sister). The broad stroke of psychosis is used to describe Ferrell. If someone has no experience with any type of cognitive disability, particularly mental illness, they may believe that anyone they meet with a cognitive disability has the capacity to do what Ferrell does (be a satanic serial killer). This belief and attitude may drive the treatment of individuals with cognitive disabilities by members of their community. The belief that cognitively disabled individuals are criminal, dangerous, "less than" other members of a community will result in marginalization and stigmatization of those individuals. As there is no evidence that the majority of individuals with a cognitive disability do fit into these stereotypes (Diefenbach 1997), nor commit more crimes due to their cognitive disability (Peterson 2014), this disparity is problematic at best, particularly in the social construction of disability.

Berger and Luckmann (1966) were among the first to acknowledge that reality is socially constructed. Social constructionists posit that the meanings and understanding that individuals have about aspects of life arise from communication with others. Social constructionism argues that persons, their self-identity, and psychological traits are social and historical constructions, not naturally occurring objects (Grodin and Lindlof 1996). How people understand things and behave toward them is based on their interactions with others. The use of language is central to this theory. The words we use, how we use them, and the actions that take place may all create meaning or connotative definitions of disability.

Burningham and Cooper (1999) believe that "all knowledge must in some sense be a social construction. No knowledge has fallen out of the sky with a label attached pronouncing 'absolute truth'" (298). The construction of knowledge by the media and viewer interpretation is an example of how reality can be created from fiction. Because language and meaning are the products of human interchange (Witkin 1999), the language used in the media gives viewers a new perspective and arena for knowledge. The media can also give new meanings to people that directly identify with fictional characters. Because many viewers will identify with certain characters with disabilities, they may watch that character for cues on how to react to and with individuals with that disability. This suggests that the institution of the media creates knowledge, which in turn affects viewers.

Renwick and partners (2014) discuss Hall's (1980) encoding/decoding framework in the context of disability representation within the media and social construction, asserting that media messages are meaningfully decoded by viewers and then societal perceptions play a role in how those messages are encoded, which then leads to dissemination to others. Therefore, if one decodes a message regarding a disability, how society has helped in the construction of understanding that disability will play a role in the impact the message has on the viewer, leading to how that message is further disseminated. This sociology of knowledge regards human reality as socially constructed (Berger and Luckmann 1966). This social construction works both ways with media representations not only informing viewers but also being informed by viewers as to what society perceives as acceptable (as Renwick et al. [2014] point out in their discussion of occupations in the media). If society deems that the treatment of certain individuals in the media should be positive then the media would be more likely to reflect that. Media sources that are intent on being thought-provoking or challenging to societal norms would be the exception here. This is one way in which we have seen groups move through Clark's four stages mentioned in the introduction. Once society deems it unacceptable for a group to be ridiculed within the media, media producers may be less likely to continue showing that type of imagery within their content.

The way in which we establish who we are and who others are is not an autonomous process. With respect to language, the self, and others, social constructionists would focus on the communication environment. People are who they are and think what they think at least in part based on knowledge contrived from communicative interactions, including the media. "The linguistic and visual representations of medicine, illness, disease and the body in elite and popular culture and medico-scientific texts are influential in the construction of both lay and medical knowledge and experiences of these phenomena" (Lupton 1994, 78). For individuals with cognitive disabilities this processing may be more complex than for those without cognitive disabilities. Olney and Kim (2001) found that the development of self for university students with cognitive disabilities included complexities such as their own definition of disabilities, coping with their limitations, and embracing their differences.

Heather Zoller and I in our (2006) study further note the social and community complications that may arise from depictions of illness and disability in the media. This social construction of disability may be significant for the disability community as well as an individual's broader social community. Kelly (2001) points out "when the community . . . responds to the impairment [disability], they are constructing a social identity (disability) that draws on a set of cultural and social understandings about illness and disability" (403). If an individual's self-identity with a disability is discordant with the community's constructed identity based on limited or inaccurate media portray's great problems can exist. Further, social identity theory highlights the use of comparison in managing identity and particularly the role that the media can play in this process (Harwood 1999). Following this idea, if individuals are continuously comparing themselves to characters within the media, yet there are few, if any, characters similar to themselves, how might this influence their perceptions of self? This may be highlighted by whether the few portrayals are perceived as positive or negative as well.

Not only can the media have an impact on the social construction of disability and as a reflection of social values, it can also play a role in the socialization and social group identity of individuals with a disability. Much of the negative stigmatization of individuals with a disability is socially constructed, and as Barnes (1991) points out, often comes from "less enlightened times." The stigmatization does not exist solely within a societal vacuum, and socialization of individuals with disabilities may be made more challenging. Kathleen Bogart (2014) discusses the managing of social identity theory by individuals with disabilities such that in order to manage the social aspect of their own identities many individuals (seemingly more so with implicit/cognitive disabilities) attempt to "pass" as someone that does not have a disability and in fact, deny their own disability. The pressure for an individual with a disability to be "normal," that is to behave as if they do not have a disability, is grounded in US culture (Englandkennedy 2008). As previous findings have shown, cognitive disabilities have been found as more common in the media landscape than physical disabilities. (This is particularly interesting as cognitive disabilities are more difficult to code, unless explicitly mentioned). Could these portrayals bring cognitive disability out of hiding? Are there characters and representations that may give individuals with cognitive disabilities someone to identify with, someone that can help change the need to hide?

As previously mentioned in chapters 1 and 2, there has been significant research examining the portrayal of the cognitive disability of mental illness in the media. There have been fewer studies examining other cognitive disabilities or the more current look into specific cognitive disabilities, but the following does show similar trends as to what has been discovered about physical disabilities. Much of the early work concentrated on mental health and mental illness within the media. In 1957, Jum Nunnally examined the mass media's portrayal of mental health, specifically looking at psychotic, neurotic, and mentally deficient behavior. The sample showed just 3.1% of the material gathered as containing information related to cognitive health. Even this percentage seemed "incidental" within the content, versus a central part of the material. They found that their media sample "emphasized the bizarre symptoms of the mentally ill" (229). This was even true for mild disorders, which seemed to come and go based on circumstance (e.g., a series of negative events could cause someone's neuroses). And, much like other presentations, findings closely followed the media model of dependency on others for cognitive health issues.

In one of the most comprehensive examinations of cognitive health in the media, Signorielli (1989), examined media content from 1969-1985. While still finding a very small population (3%), she found that 22.5% of those identified with the cognitive disability of mental illness in her sample population were seen as "good" while the remaining 77.5% were either bad (27%) or a mix of bad and good, with 72.1% of mentally ill characters hurting or killing others. Fruth and Padderud (1985) further found the overall negative and inaccurate presentation of mental illness within soap operas. Ironically, most of the soap operas they examined had psychiatrists within their cast but those perceived as mentally ill were rarely seen in therapy. Unfortunately, when shown in therapy, presentations of individuals with disabilities were usually of those beyond help or patients not willing to aid in recovery. Fruth and Padderud's analysis led to the discovery that the presentation of mental illness continued the theme of individuals engaging in negative behaviors and that treatment for cognitive health is not effective. Outside of mental illness, Wahl (et al. 2007) and Worrell (2012) also found characters with a cognitive disability to be portrayed as criminals, violent, aggressive and cruel individuals (again, these are not in line with real-life percentages of individuals engaging in such behavior).

The previously mentioned studies of Englandkennedy (2008) and Holton (2013) both address those with specific disabilities of Attention Deficit Disorder (ADD) and Asberger's, respectively. Findings within these studies show that portrayals continue to be inaccurate and in some cases "reinforce social concerns and negative stereotypes" (Englandkennedy 2008, 112). Englandkennedy (2008) found not one positive portrayal of individuals with Attention Deficit Disorder; she found that those with ADD were portrayed as maladjusted and unable to live a successful life. Holton (2013) found the media to be a stigmatizing and threatening space for those with autism. The portrayals of cognitive disabilities in the media seem to be complex in that broad, general cognitive disabilities are predominantly inaccurately and negatively portrayed, whereas specific disabilities range from outright misinformation and negativity being presented all the way to more inclusive, mostly accurate and positive portrayals (Hall and Minnes 1999). Perhaps it is easier to foster negative stereotypes of a more generalized "cognitively disabled" group than for specific disabilities such as Down syndrome.

Even for programs that receive accolades for their representations, for example Lauren Potter's character on *Glee*, there are episodes interspersed that walk the line between full inclusion and demeaning negativity. In the episode "Shooting Star," Becky brings a gun to school which, after it goes off, has the school go into lockdown. One of the teachers takes the blame for the gun "misfiring" and is fired, losing her job on Becky's behalf. One argument in support of having the character with Down syndrome bring the gun or be the "criminal" includes the continuing inclusivity of the program for Becky and her storylines. On the other side of the argument is the fear that the continued stereotype of a connection between cognitive disabilities and violence will simply be perpetuated. Of course, if no one is truly impacted by the representation of individuals with cognitive disabilities, then this would be a moot point.

MEDIA REPRESENTATIONS OF COGNITIVE DISABILITY IMPACT ON SOCIETY

Several studies have been conducted to try and ascertain the impact of the media's representation of cognitive disabilities. Again, much of the focus is on mental illness with findings showing that individuals reading news articles with a violent crime committed by an individual with mental illness increased negative attitudes toward those with mental illness (Thornton and Wahl 1996). The media encourages the public to see the mentally ill as "special, distinct and probably inferior" to others (Fruth and Padderud 1985). There is little representation or research focusing on the broader umbrella of cognitive disabilities or any of the many other areas of cognitive limitations.

Outside of fictional character portrayals of disability, Quinlan and Bates (2010) also looked at the media attention surrounding former President Bush and his frequent speech mistakes, often attributed in the media to a learning disability. This specific example speculated on the role that the media played on how society might come to understand individuals with cognitive disabilities. The fact that the media chose to ridicule Bush versus use the opportunity to further understanding of learning and cognitive disabilities directly translates to societal ridicule of those with disabilities. "This ridicule appears to be premised on an interpretation of disabilities, including learning disabilities, as bodily or cognitive differences that are deficiencies in the individual to be ridiculed" (Quinlan and Bates 2010, 9).

Most of the positive portrayals have, unsurprisingly, come from actors with a cognitive disability playing a character with the same disability. The most prevalent is that of characters with Down syndrome. Hall and Minnes

(1999) focus on the impact of television on attitudes toward individuals with Down syndrome. The experimental procedure did not rate "positive" or "negative" attitudes but asked participants to view one of three types of programs, two featuring an individual with Down syndrome (documentary and a drama) and a third as a control. The featured programs were both presented as positive representations of Down syndrome. They found that participants exhibited a stronger willingness to volunteer and greater feelings of comfort toward individuals with Down syndrome after viewing the documentary (viewers of the drama were higher than the control program as well). An interesting area here is that both presentations of the individual with Down syndrome were not of the medical model but more in line with the cultural pluralism model. So, the presentation was one of the few which showed individuals with a cognitive disability as independent and capable, yet viewers still believed there was a higher need to volunteer to help these "types" of individuals than those in the control group.

Taking a broad view of media portrayals, Walsh-Childers (2016) discusses how positive presentations in entertainment media can influence individuals to engage in positive behaviors. Looking at specific programming, Farnall and Smith (1999) also examined more positive portrayals of disabilities within the media. Three of their portrayals were of individuals with cognitive disabilities in *Rainman*, *LA Law*, and *Life Goes On*.[1] Outcomes here were mixed when examining the impact on society. Overall, there were several positive findings where participants reported perceiving that discrimination did exist for those with cognitive disabilities and they were less likely to report negative encounters with individuals with cognitive disabilities (*Rainman*). Anger and resentment of those with cognitive disabilities was significantly lower for those that viewed *Life Goes On* and fear of those with disabilities was reduced for viewers of *LA Law*. Additionally, level of comfort around those with disabilities was increased for those watching both *Rainman* and *Life Goes On*. Some of this may be a lack of transferring comfort with one disability to another, *but* for those that watched *Life Goes On* with a main character with Down syndrome, the expressed discomfort was for those that were "mentally retarded." In other words, watching this positive performance of an individual with a cognitive disability increased discomfort with individuals with cognitive disabilities.

Several studies look to see if direct experience with individuals with disabilities may mediate the effects between viewing and social construction (Chen et al. 2014). While little direct mediation has been found, it may be that indirect processing of such images is affected. Englandkennedy (2008) in her discussion of stereotyping media, reinforces the role that processing plays for media consumers. The novelty of having a character with a disability may bring the viewer more into the program and "mindful" of the content (it would be interesting to see how this works with the novelty equals negative stimuli in mere exposure research as well), but once that initial novelty wears off, "normal" viewers are likely to "lapse into mindlessness," thus the stereotypes presented would be reinforced. Going back to social cognitive theory, this mindless reinforcement may create an attitudinal or behavioral change in the viewer where stereotypes are no longer challenged. There has been further research examining the "mindful" versus "mindless" viewing of the media, of individuals following the peripheral or central routes of processing such messages. Those with cognitive disabilities are more likely to be mindful and process messages regarding cognitive disability through a central route. Therefore, messages within the media regarding cognitive disability are likely to have more of an impact on individuals that are following these attentive routes.

MEDIA REPRESENTATIONS OF COGNITIVE DISABILITY IMPACT ON INDIVIDUALS WITH A COGNITIVE DISABILITY

In studies mentioned earlier, findings focused on society as a whole, keeping in mind the processing of messages these same portrayals would theoretically have similar yet stronger effects on individuals that are cognitively disabled. However, as research has not found much of an impact for those that have direct experiences with individuals that have disabilities, would the impact actually be similar or vastly different? Thus far, there have been little to no studies comparing individuals with and without cognitive disabilities when it comes to the media's impact. It is meaningful to note that even individuals with disabilities will have varying degrees of experience with said disability. For individuals that have a disability later in life, they may still be adjusting to their disability when confronted with media portrayals of the same disability. While there are so few studies examining the impact on individuals with disabilities overall, there have been none that really look at the individual differences within disabilities as well. There have been a few significant studies of those with disabilities and their perceptions based on media representations of disability.

While Zhang and Haller (2013) do not specify types of disabilities within their sample population, their study is one of the few that takes a comprehensive view of how the media impacts the identity of individuals with disabilities. Chapter 5 mentions their finding of a positive correlation between supercrip portrayals and positive attitudes about one's own disability. However, when the media frames individuals with disabilities in negative frames as ill victims, there is an increase in their own negative attitudes about their disability. Further, their findings showed that stigmatizing images negatively portraying individuals with disabilities may lead them to believe they are "inferior to, and less precious than, an able-bodied person's life and hence hold low self-esteem about their self-identity" (330).

Kama (2004) focuses mostly on physical disabilities, and several of his findings carry over to all individuals with disabilities. The impact of the "pitiful disabled" is especially troubling for many as it reduces those with disabilities to objects—people that cannot live life without the help of others and are simply "helpless objects." Kama's participants all hated this image, frustrated and angry with this portrayal, this lack of normalcy that seems to prevail. Further studies have speculated that negative stereotypes presented may lead individuals to deny or hide their disability from the public. This may be an easier route for some with cognitive disabilities or "hidden" illnesses. Quinlan and Bates (2010), going back to learning disabilities, discuss that individuals may not disclose these to the public because they are afraid that they will be stigmatized or negatively evaluated by others. Not only does this impact how an individual may present themselves within society but it may also cause difficulty for that individual to identify as someone with a cognitive disability.

Aside from direct effects on society, one area that is presented in work such as Samsel and Perepa (2013) is that of the third-person effect occurring for some viewers. The third-person effect (Davison 1983) states that viewers may not believe the media (or another persuasive message) will have an effect on them but that it will or could potentially have an effect on others. For Samsel and Perepa studying teachers and their perceptions of media influence on themselves regarding disabilities, there were contradictions that arose, highlighting this idea. The teachers stated the concern that the media is shaping society and attitudes toward those with disabilities but did not believe that it affected them or their teaching style. In essence, they recognized the societal impact of the media when shaping attitudes and beliefs toward disability, but it didn't impact them (third-person effect). Together with the idea of social desirability, one could imagine that this may be the response of many viewers, challenging the examination of possible attitude or behavior changes regarding those with cognitive disabilities. Even in an anonymous survey one may not want to admit to feeling prejudicial or discriminatory toward others or even admit that the media may have an effect on their attitudes or beliefs.

For all disabilities, it would be remiss if this text did not further the discussion of the impact that the social construction of a disability can have on those with disabilities in connection with the impact of the media on society. Looking from a linear process, for those without cognitive disabilities there may be a direct line between the impact of the media on their own perceptions of those with disabilities and how they then treat said individuals. When it comes to personal identity, individuals with disabilities may find that the media contributes to the stigmatization of "underperformance" within their group, which in turn will lead to underperformance of those individuals, "preventing them from realizing their intellectual potential" (Zhang and Haller 2013, p. 322). Gilson and Depoy (2000) look at identity as a bond creating group affiliation. If individuals with cognitive disabilities have few people to affiliate with in real life (individuals with the same or similar disability), then they may turn to the media to fill a void. (If we include social media in the definition of "real life"; Shpigelman and Gill [2014] found that while individuals with disabilities do use Facebook for connecting to others, most of these connections are with friends and groups without disabilities; therefore, there may be more turning to traditional forms of media such as television.) Then, their cultural group of belonging may be linked to limited, inaccurate representation. Gilson and Depoy (2000) further discuss the identity of individuals with disabilities as shaped by shared experiences of being an "out group" member which may reduce the impact of stigmatization (if the "pain" is shared it is manageable). If there is no media presence to aid here, then there is no group affiliation and negative imagery may have a more significant impact (see Schiappa, Gregg and Hewes 2005 for more discussion on intergroup, specifically the parasocial contact hypothesis discussed earlier).

Discrimination against those with cognitive disabilities based on the negative attributes socially constructed can lead to negative self-fulfilling prophecies and impact an individual's self-esteem and their own abilities (Englandkennedy 2008). If society says an individual with a disability can't do something, an individual with a disability may believe this as well. As social representations of disability are created by others—including the media—to show individuals in specific ways for a purpose (Snyder and Mitchell 2006) representations can be difficult to fully understand.

Of course, as Dillon, Byrd, and Byrd (1980) point out, the addition of cognitive disabilities can add the dramatic effect to television programs necessary to keep audiences in suspense. The unpredictability of what the schizophrenic killer is going to do next can keep one on the edge of the seat. But this shouldn't necessarily exclude a conclusion with discussion or treatment options that may make for an interesting ending to the drama. As there has been so little research examining the impact of the media on individuals with cognitive disabilities, the following chapter presents a case study to offer some general insights into this area.

NOTE

1. *Life Goes On* was also the dramatic program used in the Halls and Minnes (1999) study.

Chapter Eight

A Case Study of the Media's Impact on Individuals with Cognitive Disabilities

In 1987, Willowbrook State School in New York City closed its doors. The school was the largest state-run institution for individuals with cognitive disabilities in the United States. Built for 4,000 residents in the late 1960s, there were over 6,000 confined to what Senator Robert Kennedy famously called a "snake pit" (Minnesota 2013). Dan Gunderman of the *New York Daily News* (Gunderman 2017) recently looked back at the "atrocities" of the school. Residents were mentally, physically and medically abused with allegations of medical experimentation (residents were said to have been purposefully given Hepatitis) and gross mistreatment. Geraldo Rivera in 1972 won a Peabody for his investigation and exposé in the documentary, "Willowbrook: The Last Disgrace" which Gunderman calls the impetus to a 1972 class action suit against the facility. While in 1975 the judgement was signed for the school to close, it took until the early 1980s before New York began to actively shut the institution's doors and until 1987 for the last resident to be transferred. What is perhaps most chilling is that the residents of the facility were children with cognitive disabilities that were sent to the school at a time when the government had little understanding or care regarding the treatment of individuals that were seen as different or "not normal." Fortunately, cases like Willowbrook led to widespread changes in laws and policies in regard to the treatment of individuals with cognitive disabilities. Unfortunately, many of the stigmatizations and stereotypes of the same timeframe did not change quite as drastically. Some of this may be based on the media coverage of disability.

While the media landscape may be looking up a bit in regard to the inclusion of individuals with disabilities in the media, and some scholars have found positive results on the societal and individual impacts of such

81

portrayals (Hall and Minnes 1999), there is really very little research into how these representations are impacting individuals with cognitive or intellectual disabilities. Much like within the discussion of physical disabilities, cognitive disabilities as covered within this study include intellectual disabilities, severe and persistent mental illness, and disabilities that stem from illness such as Alzheimer's or other neurological diseases. While chapter 6 presented a specific case study examining individuals that are deaf/hard of hearing, this chapter takes a broad and exploratory view of cognitive disabilities and the impact the media has on individuals with cognitive disabilities. As noted, cognitive disabilities are usually presented in the media with broad generalizations and diagnoses, but few studies have examined specific presentations as they are usually limited to one program or even one episode.

One area that has very limited research is looking into the impact of media portrayals of cognitive disabilities on those with the same or similar disabilities. One reason that this analysis is limited may be due to the lack of characters with a disability in the media. But as has been noted earlier, this shortcoming in itself can play an important role in the shaping of one's identity. Another factor may be in the difficulty of examining individuals with varying degrees of cognitive disabilities. This case study was made possible with the help of ARC of Monroe in Rochester, New York. This case study examines cognitive disability and sense of self, the role of the audience, and then specifically makes an exploratory examination of how individuals with cognitive disabilities perceive the presentation of disability in the media, who they are identifying with and how portrayals are impacting identity.

COGNITIVE DISABILITIES AND SENSE OF SELF

One's perception of self is a constructed organization of attributes, feelings, and identifications that the person takes as defining him or herself (Charmaz 1998b). For example, Murphy (1998) reports on his initial feelings about himself and his masculinity from when he was first confined to a wheelchair due to a tumor. "It was not just that people acted differently toward me, which they did, but rather that I felt differently toward myself. I had changed in my own mind, in my self-image, and in the basic conditions of my existence. It left me feeling alone and isolated, despite strong support from family and friends; moreover, it was a change for the worse, a diminution of everything I used to be" (62). He adds, "Though I may not brood over my impairment, it is always on my mind in spoken or unspoken form, and I believe this is true of all disabled people" (68). Smedema (2014) reports similarly that individuals integrate their disability as a part of their self-concepts and that in order to "accept" their disability they needed to minimize perceived losses and retain value of the abilities that they still have. This acceptance then reflects one's overall self-concept.

The sense of self of individuals with disabilities can change once they realize how others view them. Altered social interaction can cause individuals to reassess themselves and their lives. This can lead to negative interpretations of self and how one appears to other people. These concepts may be more relevant to individuals with obvious physical disabilities; however, once a cognitive disability is commonly known to an individual's family and social network the same results can ensue. Kathy Charmaz (1998a) uses an example to highlight the shock that one can feel when discovering others' views of them. "Ernest Hirsch (1977), a psychologist who had multiple sclerosis, used a wheelchair. He believed that his colleagues had hardly noticed his illness until, to his shock he discovered that he would not be permitted to practice psychotherapy because of it" (77). His perceptions of himself changed after discovering how others viewed him. Identities are formed in part by the way an individual defines, locates, and differentiates him or herself compared to others. In a timeless manner, if a person is treated with ridicule, contempt, or aversion, then his or her own ego could be diminished; his or her dignity and humanity are called into question (Murphy 1998).

THE AUDIENCE

Studies regarding the impact of the media continue to be expanded by audience studies. According to Webster (1998), "the bulk of communication research is commercial research that addresses the question of measuring audiences, rather than studying the process through which audiences reject or ingest the information presented to them" (191). More recently, Nelson and Webster (2016) move into the discussion of these large datasets and how ratings and engagement occupy much of research for marketers and media managers. Whether or not audience engagement is active or passive is a central question that has driven the study of how individuals interact with the media. Research has failed to adequately explore outside influences regarding disability on viewers and how the viewers consume the television program's messages in an everyday manner.

Ratings research has been done to determine why certain shows do as well as or as poorly as they do. Some of the earliest audience studies were designed to measure the size of radio audiences and the "reach" of print publications (McQuail 1994). Effects were looked at structurally—the size of the audiences, the social composition, the who and where of the audience. The term "structural" is used because the goal of the research is to describe the audience in terms of its composition and its relation to the social structure as a whole (McQuail 1994). This type of research is mainly used by media organizations as a form of feedback. Methods to gain this information in-clude surveys, audience diaries or television meters. More current research examines the use of social media and ratings. For example, Cheng, Wu, and Chen (2016) examine the correlation between television ratings and social media use. They found that more social media engagement with a program (i.e., posts, likes, fan page engagement) was related to Nielsen ratings. How-ever, this does not give us complete insight into the potential effects of the media.

As previously mentioned, the average American watches over four hours of television a day (Nielsen Total Audience Report Q4 2016). With this in mind, many individuals have looked at how television viewing and television programs affect their audience. The majority of studies of television effects have looked at viewpoints such as studying how television violence, crime, and racism affect people (Shrum et al. 1998). Violence on television has been studied from almost every angle imaginable. Topics that have been deemed to have more of a societal or global interest seem to be deemed more research worthy. Current research also focuses on how the violence on television may impact real-world events (Huesmann and Taylor 2006).

Examinations into the effect of violence on television are important but not the only area of research that should be of societal concern. It is short-sighted to think that other areas of research have a less significant or impor-tant impact on individuals or society. This case study builds upon the previ-ous research, adding a look into audiences that has not commonly been done before. Audience studies are complex examinations that have to look beyond simply how an audience may immediately respond to content. It is important to look at why an audience responds the way it does. Of course, how much power a media message has on an audience will at least partially depend on the attention, interpretation and use by viewers (Kitzinger 1999).

The earliest notions of stimulus-response effects within the study of mass media have become dubious. The model does not allow for audience re-sponse, which implies interaction and a learning process (McQuail 1994). The thought of individuals manipulated by an almighty mass media entity is tenuous at best. There are a number of influences that include cognitive factors, group membership, and social networks, that play a mediating role between the mass media and target audiences (Pearson 1993). More recently it has also become important to acknowledge perceived access to characters or the actors/actresses that play them. Through new technology viewers can now believe that they are in even stronger relationships with media charac-ters than in the past (see the aforementioned parasocial research). But, this knowledge about audiences is still an essential tool for media organizations (McQuail 1994). Media response theories tend to focus on the study of audiences as sets of people with unique experiences (sometimes shared) and as in charge of their own lives (to some degree).

As media viewers are perceived as active in the process of media consumption, the uses and gratifications theory focuses on the choice, reception, and response of the media audience. Early scholars of this approach (e.g. Herzog 1944) studied motives for content choices of television viewers and what satisfaction they were looking for from the media. Abelman and Atkin (2000) highlight three basic tenets of the uses and gratification theory: 1) viewers are goal directed in their behavior; 2) they are active media users; and 3) they are aware of their needs and select media to gratify these needs (1444). In attempting to gratify these needs the audience is also shaping their own views of themselves and the world. Further theoretical understanding underscores the importance of shaping meaning within these contexts.

In the 1930s, Mead laid the foundations of the symbolic interactionist approach. A few decades later, Blumer coined the phrase. Blumer (1969) believes that symbolic interactionism rests on three premises. The first is that human beings act toward things on the basis of the meanings that the things have for them. Second, the meanings of such things arise from the social interaction one has with one's peers. Lastly, these meanings are modified through an interpretative process used by the person in dealing with the things he or she encounters. These assumptions are very similar to theoretical assumptions discussed earlier, again supporting the idea that our construction of meaning does not exist in a vacuum.

This perspective emphasizes the meanings and intentions people construct through their interactions (Charmaz 1998b). Pertaining to television, this theory posits that the media contains symbols that carry meaning, yet the meanings must be learned. They are learned by interactions the audience has in their daily life as well as what they "learn" from viewing. So, the individual is not only acted upon but in deciphering meaning they are the actor as well (Webster 1998). Many media consumers are learning about cognitive disabilities based on symbolic meanings communicated in the media. This is meaningful to this case study because of the implications revolving around learning from the media, self-identity, and social interactions.

As has been noted, the media presents viewers with great opportunities to learn about others or even ourselves. However, if one cannot relate to a character with the same or similar disabilities in the media, there may be an impact on construction of one's personal identity (Kelly 2001). The ability to identify with characters is linked to the development of self-identity (Cohen 2001). The media and identification help to construct the meaning of disability and societal attitudes. Subsequently, societal attitudes play a direct role in how individuals with a disability are treated by others. Therefore, not only is it important to examine the portrayal of disability within the media, it is also important to examine how those with disabilities 1) perceive the reported lack of portrayals in the media 2) identify with characters with disabilities and 3) are constructing identities based on these portrayals and identifications.

Much like within chapter 6, I found the best way to examine these opportunities was through primary research. Specifically, the following exploratory research questions were examined: How do individuals with cognitive disabilities perceive the presentation of disability within the media? Who are people with cognitive disabilities identifying with within the media? How (if at all) have portrayals of disabilities impacted the identity of those with cognitive disabilities?

METHOD

Procedure

In an effort to create a full and diverse sample of individuals with cognitive disabilities, I reached out to several non-profit organizations, or their affiliates in a large Northeastern city, that provide services for those with disabilities. I was able to meet with personnel of various facilities and learn about the clients as well as the perceptions of the media by those that work and volunteer at the organizations. Personnel at the various locations were asked to reach out to individuals that may be able to participate in one-on-one interviews. While this convenience sample limits the generalizability of the case study, it was important to be able to identify individuals that would be able to participate in the interview process. Through this process a number of individuals were identified that not only had an interest in media but were also interested enough in discussing it with me. Limits were not placed on cognitive ability of each participant, allowing for a wide range of cognitive disabilities to be represented in a limited sample.

Each participant was given a consent form (after IRB approval) in advance of the scheduled interview date and was asked to sign or have a guardian sign the form. Each facility then scheduled participants for me to meet with in one-on-one interviews. Interviews were scheduled back to back with a staff member bringing participants to the interview room. Some interviews required a staff member to remain to either translate or help facilitate discussion (for example, one participant used a text-to-speech program. The staff member held the participant's arm up so they were able to type their replies.) Each interview was audiotaped to ensure accuracy of quotes. At the conclusion of each interview participants received a small gift for their time (doughnuts and a pen or pencil from a local university).

Measures

Each interview began with the respondent sharing their age. In some instances, the individual was unsure of their exact age so they gave their best approximation. Each participant was cognitively disabled and some individuals also had a physical disability. Based on cognitive differences, while participants were asked the same initial questions, variations based on level of understanding were often used to try and elicit an answer. The reported measures are of the initial questions asked to all participants.

Participants were asked general questions regarding their media watching habits including frequency, favorite programs and movies. To determine how individuals with cognitive disabilities perceive the role of disability within the media, participants were asked a series of questions regarding the characters they see in the media. For example, participants were asked, "Do you know of any characters on television that have the same/similar disability as yours?" and "What do you think of that character? Is the portrayal accurate? Inaccurate?" Often questions had to be reworded to facilitate understanding, so additional questions such as what they like best and least about certain characters were also asked.

In order to ask about identification, participants were asked who they felt they were "most like" in the media. Further, they were asked for their favorite characters from television or movies. To examine how identities may be affected by the identification with such characters, participants were asked questions such as, "Do you ever compare yourself to the [favorite or any] character? If yes, what do you think? If no, why do you think you don't do that?" and "How does viewing the media make you feel about yourself?" Further follow-up questions were asked in various ways depending on the cognitive abilities of each participant to ascertain their perceptions of themselves and if they felt the media had an impact on their self-identity. [1]

FINDINGS

A total of 14 individuals participated in the case study. Participants had various developmental, cognitive, and in some cases physical disabilities. The participants also ranged in cognitive abilities from low to medium to high functioning. While the sample size was small for completely generalizable data, the sample was diverse in age, sex and race. Interviews ranged from 14 to 50 minutes in length with an average of 25 minutes. There was an obvious relationship between degree of perceived function and length of interview such that individuals that were lower functioning answered many questions with yes/no responses or chose not to answer some questions. (Open-ended questions were used to reduce acquiescence; however, this may have resulted in more misunderstandings of how to reply to questions.) It is common for a higher frequency in yes/no responses as more open-ended responses can be more cognitively demanding for those with intellectual disabilities (Perry 2004).

Media exposure ranged from very limited—respondents that watched very little television/movies and had little experience with printed media—to individuals that had very high levels of exposure with upward of six hours of media use within a weekday. Several participants reported higher levels of use on weekends. The majority of respondents regularly watched the evening news and there were few reports of viewing current programming with activity ranging more toward programs that were older and not in the first run on television (favorite shows included *The Three Stooges, Dr. Quinn Medicine Woman, Buffy the Vampire Slayer,* and cartoons).

The first research question[2] looked to examine how individuals with disabilities perceive the role of disability within the media. Three themes were prevalent in the participants' discussions of disability in the media. First, almost unanimously, respondents reported little to no knowledge of individuals with disabilities in the media. Second, there was a mix of negative and positive portrayals within the media. Finally, most participants would like to see more people like "them" on television.

In the discussion regarding the number of individuals with disabilities in the media, it was very difficult for most respondents to think of an example of a character with a disability. Of those that were able to name individuals with disabilities in the media, they were more likely to mention those with physical disabilities (i.e., Artie from *Glee*). Two movies were mentioned: one of them, *The Ringer*, has a man posing as developmentally disabled in order to win at the Special Olympics. Several of the supporting characters are actors with various disabilities. Sara (female, mid-30s) did enjoy seeing characters that she believed had a disability. Conversely, however, she didn't believe that others would enjoy the film and would think, "why did they make a movie with someone with special needs?" The second film, *Avatar*, has a character in a wheelchair that is able to walk in his "avatar" form. Ivan (male, mid-50s), a big fan of the film, reported this as the only disability he's ever seen in the media.

When it comes to the types of portrayals, there were a mix of negative and positive portrayals perceived by participants. For some the level of acting/representation was frustrating in its inaccuracy. Sam, mid-20s, pointed out "you can tell they are just acting it out . . . that's a little bit frustrating" and "you don't know what you are doing to portray this person or this character," expressing his frustration in how some of the characters with disabilities were portrayed. For others, the acting itself was less a problem than the actors not actually having disabilities, the disability drag: "people, change the people," said Gina, female, mid-40s.

Participants would like to see the positive portrayals highlighted on television but are not adverse to seeing the negative aspects as well, the "good and the bad" to make television more like the real world (Sara, female, mid-30s). For some participants like Laura (mid-40s), "The media doesn't understand that we have feelings too. Yes, we may have DS [Down syndrome], we may have CP [Cerebral Palsy], we may have behavioral stuff but we are still human beings and we still have feelings." But as Jenny, female, early 50s points out, "I've never seen anyone that's a murderer . . . that's good, I guess."

Most participants would like to see more characters with disabilities in the media. Vince, male, mid-50s, stated that he would "like to see more people like me" on television. "I would like to see more people [with disabilities], I'd like to see us on TV," said Sara, female, mid-30s. Jenny, female, early 50s, agreed, pointing out that it would likely be harder for people to learn about disabilities when they are not seen within the media. And, maybe if there are more characters on television with disabilities others "will think twice when they see someone in real life with a disability" (Sam, male, mid-20s).

The second research question looked to see who individuals with disabilities were identifying with within the media. Not one respondent chose a character with disabilities. Replies ranged from the comedic characters, dramatic actors, and even professional athletes.

> "I am that guy from the new sitcom [Ken Marino from *Marry Me*]. I think, I would do that, yeah, I can relate to that."—Sam, male, mid-20s.

> "Mindy from *Mork and Mindy* is me."—Laura, female, mid-40s.

> "Professional wrestlers . . . they are just like me"—Lucas, male, mid-50s.

Several individuals identified or compared themselves to cartoon characters such as Scooby-Doo or, "Curious George . . . he's wild, just like me. . . . His friends tell him he can't do things and he needs help." (Jenny, female, early 50s).

While John, male, mid-20s, couldn't think of anyone in the media that he did identify with, he believed the closest were football players as he would loved to have played himself. This was a trend for some of the discussions in which individuals didn't clearly identify with anyone but they did discuss characters to whom they would slightly compare themselves or want to be like. These comparisons most frequently discussed positive attributes of characters that individuals saw within themselves. "Jane Seymour, Dr. Quinn, is my idol. . . . I compare myself to her . . . we both have nice smiles and are nice to other people," Sara, female, mid-30s. In some cases, it was individuals that participants would like to "be like," "I would like to be the girl on 7th Heaven [Jessica Biel], I would like to be like her . . . she's smart, she has a gorgeous husband . . . " (Michelle, female, mid-40s).

In discussing these characters there was some dissatisfaction that participants could not identify with characters, "I wish that more characters that had disabilities or portrayed as disabled were more relatable," said Sam, male, mid-20s. However, there were some that pointed out relief in the lack of "similar" characters as negative portrayals would "make me feel bad" and there were concerns expressed that such portrayals would cause others to make comparisons and as Sara pointed out others would "expect me to be like the characters on TV."

The final research question explored how the portrayals of disabilities may have impacted the identity of those with disabilities. While no participants directly identified with characters with disabilities, there was discussion regarding the portrayals of disabilities themselves. For some, positive portrayals helped them to feel better about themselves, "I like when TV programs show how people with disabilities can do things . . . seeing characters do things that I can't do makes me want to try and do them" (Sara, female, mid-30s). Conversely, she feels bad when she "can't do it—it is hard [I] think others will judge if I can't do it." Jenny, female, mid-50s, says that it makes her feel good when she sees people "going through the same things she is going through." If more people needed help on TV it would be easier for her when she needs help. Individuals interviewed had a sense of being "invisible" within most of society. Many individuals were identifying as "unimportant," as if people with disabilities were not important enough to be seen in the media.

When it comes to interactions with others, some participants report feeling stigmatized based on portrayals or lack thereof in the media. For Sam, he feels that some friends treat him differently based on people they compare him to in the media, and hopes that in all portrayals people remember, "we are still people at the end of the day; it's not like we are stupid or not educated. We know a lot more than people give us credit for." Negative portrayals can "make you kind of angry" and he worries that these portrayals will make others "rather than being sympathetic more dismissive." Many participants discussed the need for reminders that they are "people first."

The final question of each interview asked participants, "If you could say one thing about the representation of disability in the media, what would it be?" Responses seemed to focus on two main ideas—the first, to show people with disabilities. One participant repeated many times, "Please tell others about us," believing that highlighting those with disabilities in the media would bring those with disabilities into the light. The second is the need for respect, respect from others and respect from the media and the idea that individuals with disabilities are people first:

Don't count us out. . . . I've been fighting my whole life to prove that I'm just like everyone else, because we are. I think that sometimes the media gets it wrong and sometimes they get it right and I would hope that for the future the media continues to get it right. . . . It doesn't matter what our handicap is, we all want respect. . . . We are people first (Sam, male, mid-20s).

DISCUSSION

It is disheartening to see that in the decades of research examining disability in the media, there has been little growth in numbers of individuals with disabilities on television. While societal policies may be increasing individuals' awareness of disabilities in "real life," there is still limited information in the media. If television is a primary resource for health information for those not health-oriented (Dutta-Bergman 2004) or seeking specific information, then it may not matter how much policy change we see in the real world if the fictional world still does nothing for inclusion. Uniformly, participants in this study believed that more people understanding about disabilities would make their lives easier.

Much of the discussions in this exploratory study supported previous findings and speculation in regard to portrayals of disabilities in the media. The low percentage of findings regarding representation of disability (Bond 2008; Worrell 2012) seems to manifest in the fact that even individuals with first-hand experience with disability have trouble naming characters with disabilities in the media. This lack of representation was discussed in terms similar to cultivation analysis and social cognitive theory discussed in chapter 3. The lack of representation makes things harder for some individuals with disabilities because not only are people unaware of the existence of said disabilities but they don't "learn" how to treat people with said disabilities. (Interestingly, each participant truly did put people first when identifying with characters. Even though Michelle didn't truly believe she was like Jessica Biel's character, she wanted to embody the positive qualities that she displays as a person on the program.)

Zhang and Haller (2013) found that individuals with disabilities report the few individuals with disabilities seen in the media as "supercrips, disadvantaged or ill victims" (329). The interviews brought about very similar ideas. Participants, while not describing specific accounts, did feel that the media was not helping improve current stereotypes or stigmatizations. The call for respect and understanding that people with disabilities "still have feelings" would support the idea of a mostly negative representation of disabilities in the media. If portrayals were abundant and positive, individuals would not feel disrespected or invisible. And, like Kama (2004), even the supercrip portrayals were not always seen as positive, with respondents fearing stigmatization from comparisons to characters that may be able to perform in ways they cannot.

How does this all shape identities? For this sample, disability specific portrayals in the media did not seem to play a role in their creation of self-identity. However, the lack and types of portrayals did make individuals feel invisible, hurt, and disrespected. These feelings could have an impact on self-identity, increasing feelings of stigmatization and generally, "being looked at like a freak" (Laura, female, mid-40s) for individuals with disabilities. These limits may not allow an individual to fully realize their own identity.

As Cohen (2001) points out, the ability to identify with characters is linked to the development of self-identity. If there is no one to identify with, individuals with disabilities may struggle in constructing their true identity and in effect suffer from low self-esteem or low self-efficacy. Participants themselves were recognizing this need as many seemed to believe that they would feel better about themselves if they were able to see positive portrayals of individuals with disabilities in the media. There was also an understanding that more people "like them" in the media could lead to more awareness of disabilities, more understanding from others, and more support whether from services or simply people in their lives, bringing about even more positive change.

CONCLUSION

As the media landscape remains relatively scarce with representation and individuals with disabilities find few characters to identify with, one has to wonder why—why so little representation. In 1997, Mattel introduced a Barbie doll in a wheelchair, "Share a smile Becky." The original doll had to be modified with shorter hair (to avoid snagging it in the wheels) and a smaller wheelchair (to fit in the Barbie dream house). The revised doll had great sales for the company but when complaints were made that the doll didn't fit in the dream house elevator rather than upgrading the home, Mattel dumped the doll (Ams Van 2011). Are media producers metaphorically "dumping" disability roles in the same way? Scholars and researchers utilize large samples and hours of media viewing to find little representation of individuals with a disability in the media so it is not surprising that individuals with disabilities themselves cannot find such characters.

While it may be difficult to accurately assess some of these concepts in a population where cognitive ability can vary so widely (for example, high-functioning respondents easily appeared to understand most questions asked and provided lengthy replies, lower-functioning individuals tended to stick to yes/no replies with little to no indication of understanding), even more research needs to be conducted in this area. Interviews, experiments, surveys, focus groups are all a part of future research in this area. There is a need for more data to be collected for more generalizable results and even more clarity in understanding the perceptions of portrayals and possible impacts on identity. Finally, it is important to note that more research in this area can help to carry out Ivan's plea, "Please tell others about us."

NOTES

1. I would be remiss if I did not at least mention how much fun these interviews were. I am extremely grateful to everyone that participated and shared their insights with me.

2. For quote attributions, names have been changed and sex and age range were listed to provide a bit more context to some quotes.

III

What Can the Media Do?

We've seen what the media is showing and what the media is doing but there has been little discussion about the positive capabilities of the media. What can the media do? The book's final chapter discusses suggestions to media producers, health practitioners, and more as to how we might go about avoiding, fixing, or helping in the context of the lack of media portrayals, inaccurate representations, and impacts on society and individuals with disabilities. Can the media as well as supportive others change the stigmatization of individuals with disability? How can understanding what is in the media aid health practitioners and caregivers when working with individuals with disabilities? What role can an audience, both with and without disabilities, play if the limited, negative representation persists or if we see a surplus of super-crips? While specific calls to action are provided, more general guiding ideas are discussed as well.

Chapter Nine

Suggestions and Tips for the Media and the Rest of Us

When I was a kid I loved Jo from the television show *Facts of Life*. I liked her because she was tough, smart, and funny. I really disliked Blair. she was portrayed as less intelligent and shallow. As I got a little older I realized why I had such a dislike for her character—she was blonde! She was the epitome of everything that one made fun of regarding stereotyping blonde women— dumb, silly, and frivolous. Why would that bother me so much? I am blonde too. I realized that I was afraid that not only would I become a teenager like her but that other people would think I was like her character, that I too would be dumb, silly, frivolous. Fortunately, I am none of those things (well, perhaps silly at times), but I have not been immune to blonde jokes my entire life. While this is a facetious example of the impact the media played in my own life, it highlights the idea that even one simple and shallow presentation within the media played a role in my own identity.

It seems safe to say, based on the previous research cited within this text, that the representation of disability in the media is inadequate, inaccurate, mostly negative, and may have significant impact on society's treatment of individuals with disabilities (particularly when it comes to stereotyping and stigmatization) as well as significant impact on individuals with those disabilities and their identity. Much like the newspapers' calls to end "invisibility" within the media, scholars have been calling on media producers to increase both the representation and positive portrayals of individuals with disabilities, to listen to Ivan's plea and tell others about individuals with disabilities and to do so in a responsible manner. But, media organizations are not alone in shouldering the responsibility of how the media impacts society or individuals. Policy makers, health professionals, and caregivers and all viewers can play a role in disability in the media.

MEDIA PRODUCERS

Media producers are traditionally seen as the "bad guys" within scholarly research into the detrimental effects of content (Seale 2003). This is due in part to the fact that consumers spend over 11 hours a day interacting with some type of media content, and almost five of those hours watching television (Nielsen Total Audience Report Q4 2016). After all, if the media producers didn't allow the content to air, then we wouldn't have to worry, right? But, a number of producers utilize outside advisors, experts in the field for anything that is "not normal" within the program. These technical advisors "inject a dose of reality into make-believe" (Miller 2016). Medical dramas such as *Chicago Med* and *Grey's Anatomy*, both have practicing physicians on staff to review scripts, assist in terminology and even show characters the proper way to hold medical instruments. David Salzberg is a physicist and astronomer that helps keep *The Big Bang Theory* as accurate as possible and writes all of the formulas seen on the screen. Former police officers, military officers, computer scientists, FBI agents, lawyers, pilots, nurses, CEOs, and more have all lent a hand to the media to ensure as much accuracy and realism to storylines as possible. Some of the programs discussed in this text have also utilized advisors to try and accurately portray an individual with a disability. Max Burkholder, Max on the show *Parenthood*, worked with a doctor specializing in working with children with autism. *Law and Order* also frequently has doctors on set to help when medical cases arise. *Criminal Minds*, full of the serial killing insane, has a criminal profiler on staff as a technical advisor (see Rosenburg 2013).

Credit where it is due, this is a huge step in presenting some level of accuracy when it comes to the portrayal of disability in the media. On the flipside, what's missing from the list of advisors? First, shows that have characters with disabilities don't always utilize advisors, particularly if the actor has a disability. Lauren Potter is a great actress on *Glee* but producers mainly rely on her abilities to be representative of an entire population of individuals with Down syndrome. And, as an actor she is not consulted regarding storylines or how others discuss her disability. *Switched at Birth*, on the other hand, does have a translator on set and, as noted, many of the actors are deaf, but they have no deaf writers or directors/producers on staff. Barnes (1991) points out the problem of images of disability in the media being created and produced by people without disabilities. To the best of my knowledge, there are no technical advisors with the same disability as a character being utilized in the production process of television programs.[1] While the use of doctors may minimize the inaccuracy of specific information, first-hand knowledge from individuals that have a portrayed disability throughout the process from writing to directing would go a long way in increasing accuracy and minimizing negative stereotypes.

Not only do media practitioners have a moral obligation to show accurate representations of disability in the media, but these portrayals should also be balanced. As has been mentioned, disability drag is problematic and can be solved by having actors and actresses who actually have a disability to play the character with a disability. While this practice will likely not change the type of character ("crazy criminal" or socially awkward obsessive compulsive), at least the disability itself will be more accurately represented. Chapter 1 mentioned the Media Access Office (MAO) in Los Angeles. There is also the Performers with Disabilities Tri-Union Committee of the Screen Actors Guild who put forward the Inclusion in the Arts and Media of People with Disabilities campaign, working for more media presence and inclusion for actors with disabilities. Utilizing a readily available resource for producers would allow for an increase in realism of portrayals. But, as mentioned, this would not fully provide balance as character type may not be realistic or positive.

An additional option would be to have more than one character with the same disability within a program. It is understood that the cannibalistic serial killer presents an interesting storyline and a bad guy for the heroes to capture, but perhaps in the same program have one of the "good" guys also be schizophrenic or portray an individual that has a cognitive disability as having a "normal" lifestyle. Of course, doing this across time may not be completely viable for the episodic nature of television, but if mere exposure effect is accurate the repeated exposure will only increase positive feelings, and further the congruity principle that an additional positive portrayal would allow for any negative attitudes to at least potentially be mitigated by the addition of the positive portrayal. If that isn't functionally or financially viable, providing information or even a positive public service announcement at the end of an episode that contains a negative, stereotypical portrayal may help create a balance for the viewer. Changes may cost money and media producers must respond to the bottom line; therefore, there is a need to clearly examine and promote profitability or at the least, no increase in expenses for such changes.

Of course, it is easy to be on the outside of the media industry looking in, and one realizes that most media portrayals of disability are not intended to change perceptions of people with disabilities or even to raise awareness. The portrayals are usually to further a plot or add drama. But if producers can realize that they (and consumers) should be as concerned with portrayals of disability as they are with whether Dr. House can properly hold a scalpel, properly constructed "media representations of characters with disabilities may be able to provide new, more humanizing representations of people with disabilities for the public and to counteract negative models and stereotypes" (Englandkennedy 2008, 95). More positive representations could do a lot for society as well as individuals with disabilities. Television has been shown to be an effective prosocial tool (see discussions on Entertainment-Education) and this can extend into decision-making arenas for policy makers and voters.

When it comes to journalists, as media producers, understanding the occurrence of image echoes and how what and how they write, even about fictional characters, may have an impact on individuals with disabilities is important. There are current suggested policies regarding how to write about individuals with disabilities as outlined in chapter 2. However, there are no policies in place to enforce suggestions or codes of ethics. Currently, there is a push to examine news media more critically and be more aware of "fake news." This push could include more than just concern about the presentation of political facts but also more overall critically understanding that the information presented in the news is not necessarily accurate or that of a social majority. It is simply a recitation of information written by an individual.

The Society of Professional Journalists (SPJ) may also be tapped to more concretely lay out ethical treatment of individuals, including how stories are written and the language used. A principle within the SPJ code of ethics includes the idea that one should "Minimize Harm. Ethical journalism treats sources, subjects, colleagues and members of the public as human beings deserving of respect" (SPJ Code of Ethics 2017). While good in theory, even the bullet points under this principle include vague statements such as, "Consider cultural differences in approach and treatment." Writers of such codes can do more to provide solid foundations for these codes and then take perhaps a more aggressive stance themselves and with policy makers in suggesting and/or reinforcing instances that go against said codes with censure, at a minimum.

While not necessarily media producers, organizations hosting social media platforms need to be cognizant of the reinforcing impact that some posts, pages, tweets, images, may have on their participants. Often one might believe that it is simply one picture, and the impact will be limited, but understanding that our media consumption does not occur in isolation would be important. Also, increasing accessibility and ease for individuals with disabilities to connect with media content, including virtual groups and communities, must continue to be examined, particularly as social media is a great avenue for individuals to be agents for their own change, which may also reach policy makers and voters.

POLICY MAKERS AKA THE GOVERNMENT

Writing this text today versus even two years ago, makes this a difficult charge. How does one make suggestions regarding the role that policy makers may play in disability in the media when the sitting president has been charged with mocking a reporter with a disability on national television[2] and millions are concerned about losing funding for basic services? First, let's look at some of the policies in place that may play a role in the representation of disability in the media. The Americans with Disabilities Act has already been mentioned as providing more equality for individuals with disabilities, particularly as the Act prohibits discrimination and allows for "mainstreaming." Additionally, the ADA provides information speaking on behalf of accurate and positive media portrayals and inclusion for actors as well as writers and producers that have disabilities (ADA Legacy Project 2017). There are also policies focusing on more specific access for individuals with disabilities, such as the 21st Century Communications and Video Accessibility (CCTVA) Act of 2010, mentioned in chapter 1. Not only does the CCTVA Act play a role in requiring closed captioning for certain media outlets, the Act also requires services such as requiring access to mobile web browsers for individuals that are blind or visually impaired (FCC 2010). Increases in any type of mainstreaming in the "real world" or in the mediated environment, big or small, can go a long way in reducing any perceived stigmatizing "otherness" for individuals with disabilities.

Advertisers are required to follow Federal Trade Commission policies regarding false advertising and unfair or deceptive acts, whereas other forms of media have limited restrictions. While the Federal Communications Commission does forbid broadcasting of material deemed as "obscene" on public broadcast airwaves, other policies protect the writing of fictional narratives. Freedom of expression allows writers and producers to essentially come up with any storyline or character of interest and the government can do nothing about it. While this text is not advocating for government regulations over television content, perhaps a checks and balance system advocating for equality in messages (positive representations should be equal to the negative in the course of presentation, particularly for individuals of minority status) would allow for some stability of presentation. Torbjorn von Krogh (2010) focused on European government but makes universal suggestions for change. The government can ask for self-regulation from the media, remind the media of the social responsibility it has, or they can remind citizens of the power they also have over the media—in essence, citizen participation in the regulation of the media.

Perhaps there could be consideration of expansion to the Children's Television Act of 1990 or the Telecommunications Act of 1996, realizing that concern should not be limited to the effects of images of sex and violence. The Children's Television Act requires broadcasters to serve the educational needs of children under 16 years of age by airing at least three hours of educational or information programming per week. As these programs target children, the Act could be expanded to the over 16 market, requiring educational and information programming targeting adults at the same rate. There is a significant amount of research on Entertainment-Education, even reaching out to adults that would support this idea.[3]

Policy makers and government officials would also need to understand the importance of organizations such as the American Association of People with Disability or the Arc of the United States. Several organizations mentioned throughout this text work tirelessly for the rights of individuals with disabilities. Government funding to help support these groups has been imperative. Keeping said funding and allowing organizations the resources to fight stigmatization and stereotypes through their messages can help provide a counter to any negative representations. Of course, many of these policies and organizations may not have the proper time or funding to aid in regulation of content or combat negative messages, and additional funding may impact resources for caregivers.

CAREGIVERS AND HEALTH PRACTITIONERS (INCLUDING HEALTH COMMUNICATORS)

When conducting research for the case study in chapter 7, I ran across many caregivers for individuals with cognitive disabilities that were excited about understanding the media's impact on their clients. One of the reasons was the difficulty that they had understanding the daily lives of individuals with cognitive disabilities.[4] Their hope was that I could uncover some of the issues related to media consumption that might provide insight into the lives of their clients who, after all, like the US average, likely spend up to five hours a day with television on a regular basis. After further discussions and reporting to them on my findings, some of the biggest surprises were that individuals were even aware of the lack of content. Some individuals with severe cognitive disabilities were able to articulate, albeit sometimes with difficulty, the feelings of frustration of not only being an "other" in their daily lives but also in the fictional world. It is one thing to be singled out for ridicule in isolated incidents; it is another to feel that most of society, at least the portion of society seen in the media, believes the stereotypes. Caregivers were equipped to handle the "real-life" stigmas but had never thought about perceptions perpetuated by the media content.

Caregivers come in many shapes and sizes, some trained to work with individuals with disabilities and some family members that are dealing with very specific cases. For some working across individuals with a variety of disabilities, generalized knowledge about the representation and impact of the media would be, at the least, helpful. It would therefore be important for scholars and scholarly publishers to seek out this audience for input as well as educational purposes. While many clinical programs might include a component on patient/caregiver communication or on understanding cultural differences, there is little work done to discuss the influence of the external factor of the media. Increasing education in this area through courses or training regarding disability and the media could significantly aid in understanding. For "untrained" caregivers, usually family members, health professionals would need to be advocates for media understanding and at the least have discussions with caregivers as well as individuals with disabilities regarding the media's potential impact. Further, Renwick and associates (2014) discuss the environmental and social barriers that may be constructed by the media, such as employment and educational contexts that may be (hopefully unknowingly) "maintained or reinforced by practitioners." No one is immune to the media's influence. The knowledge of how caregivers themselves may be affected and how that may play a role in their own perceptions of individuals with disabilities is important.

Larger organizations can also do their part as health practitioners. Englandkennedy (2008) points out that groups can provide media makers with lists of experts to serve as advisors for programs. While it would be preferable for a media outlet to engage experts prior to production beginning, organizations can also be proactive once an individual with a disability has been introduced on a program. Englandkennedy also points out the need for organizations to take strong stances regarding stereotyped images and misinformation in the media—position papers, press releases, communication with media producers and journalists with a strong message that full inclusion doesn't mean only presentations with the potential for stigmatizing. The MAO could not only continue advocating but also start demanding the reduction of disability drag. For example, going back to *Ironside*, showrunners reported that it would have been too costly to hire an actor in a wheelchair for the part as they wanted to incorporate flashback scenes to before the character's injury (Rosenburg 2013). Perhaps it is only the cynical that might wonder about the discrepancy between the famous Blair Underwood's salary and that of a lesser known actor already in a wheelchair utilizing a few computer-generated images.

The portrayal of disability in the media can also impact how issues are discussed. For example, if individuals with cognitive disabilities are identifying with a "supercrip" on television, maybe they can't articulate why they are getting so frustrated with the inability to perfect a skill—could it be linked to a character they are identifying with on television? Being able to specifically point to and understand the exposure to such messages allows one to address specific needs. Rather than not understanding exactly why Ivan is frustrated with his lack of mobility seemingly out of the blue, a discussion of recent media exposure and the possible comparisons going on may start a conversation about the differences between fictional and non-fictional media and differences between fictional representations and reality. Further, if individuals have more access to media coverage or information counter to representations, they may be able to point individuals with disabilities in those directions.

For health communication practitioners, it may be possible to create health campaigns that would combat negative media stereotypes and reduce possible stigmatization of individuals with disabilities. For example, the aforementioned public service announcements or other materials can generate knowledge. Across the board, increases in knowledge benefits the lives of individuals with disability services. As previously mentioned, concern about the government sector and changes being made to federal and state budgets have included freezing or cutting disability services. Being able to effectively communicate messages that will educate policy makers and voters on any discrepancies that may be affecting their decision-making will be extremely important.

AUDIENCE

Throughout the years, the media have played a pervasive role in society. We have seen stories that dramatize suffering and overcoming it. Real life and fiction is increasingly becoming blurred and audiences are becoming more inundated with messages. Television is a very visual medium and for many seeing is believing. We deal with real-life situations whenever we turn on the news; we've seen these same situations depicted dramatically on shows like *Law and Order*. Most people who are old enough remember where they were when 9/11 happened; others remember where they were when any of the Starks were killed on *Game of Thrones*. Others can remember when their favorite actor died, killing their character off a favorite show or movie, blurring the lines between fiction and reality. The real lives of "ordinary" people are highlighted on reality shows like *Survivor* or *Big Brother*. Fictional representations of pain, injury and suffering are common from soap operas to *Grey's Anatomy*.

As an audience, we know that when we watch a television program we may see people being hurt, people contracting illnesses, and even people dying. In many cases the programs we watch are not seen as fiction but as representative of real life (Philo and Henderson 1999). When our favorite characters have been killed right before our eyes, some people cry over the loss of a "friend" on television. On rare occasions, we may see a character suffer an illness, car accident, beating, rape, or something equally devastating that lasts more than one episode. We watch week after week to cheer the character on to good health and happier times. In most television shows the character is treated by doctors in hospitals using the latest technology and fast acting drugs and they have a full recovery (Lupton 1994).

When it comes to disability in the media it is clear that those television programs along with the news presented regarding characters with disability can have a significant impact on an audience. By educating audiences through texts such as this, scholarly research, advocacy group communications, health campaigns and more, they will gain the ability to more critically process the messages seen. Singer and Singer (1998) advocate for starting this education with children and media literacy programs in schools. Once a clear understanding takes place that images in the media are not necessarily representative, potentially inaccurate and/or misleading messages will begin to lose their impact.

Also, as the media is often a reflection of society, audience members can use the tools available to speak to media outlets regarding the presentation of disability in the media. Everything from letter writing to instant feedback through social media can promote change.[5] Following a live Twitter event for a program? Ask questions about new or unclear character portrayals. Getting into a Reddit AMA with a media producer? Challenge them to defend negative portrayals of minorities in their programs. Worried about others being impacted by the media's presentations? Perform the positive behaviors that should be emulated by others. In 2016, *The Washington Post* covered the proliferation of the Twitter hashtag #CripTheVote to try and increase media coverage and the political discussion surrounding disability issues. This "simple" social media campaign, perpetuated by "the audience," was reported on through multiple traditional news outlets and gave voice to the media content of the coverage of disability and the 2016 election.

While researchers have alternated between the active and passive audience description for almost a century, little current work has examined the active audience in terms of their power over the media. In fact, new trends into examining "fake news" and the impact of social media has made the audience seem even more passive than ever. But, if McQuail (1994) and Katz (1980) are still correct, the power that the media has fluctuates based on the strength of the audience. Of course, not relying on fictional images for health information is also important for audience growth in factual knowledge and to reduce misinformation. With little knowledge, things like negative stereotyping within the media go unquestioned and may become normal. This allows stigma to grow as these unquestioned stereotypes are "more easily and unreflectively enacted" (Englandkennedy 2008). If an image, however, does not conform to preconceived stereotypes the impact on a viewer may be minimized.

In a review of this text I was asked about a section on "what the disabled can do." As I reflected on this comment my first instinct was to simply say, "Well, they are part of the audience and can follow the same suggestions." But that is not enough. After all, if I am advocating for the voice of those with disabilities to be heard, I should also ask those with disabilities to be the loudest. It is important for individuals to claim their own agency, to under-stand they are capable of creating change and influencing important aspects of their lives. So, yes, follow the advice to general audiences regarding feedback and other processes to be heard. Speak out! Continue to fight. Reach out to advocacy groups to discuss the media and celebrate the positive, accurate representations. Don't just dismiss inaccurate or negative portray-als—speak out against them and take control of the story.

CONCLUSION

When thinking about how to conclude this text, I made a note to myself to "recap the good, the bad, and the ugly and then make final pithy comments." Taking my own advice: The good—representation of disability in the media seems to be growing, if only slightly, across media platforms. The number of outlets available for media consumption gives more access than even ten years ago. Some programs are bringing on main characters with disabilities where the disability is not the central focus of the character (e.g., Dr. Al Robbins on *CSI*). There are shows where almost an entire cast is individuals with disabilities, such as the A&E show *Born This Way* that centers on seven young adults with Down syndrome and their lives. With any increase, indi-viduals with disabilities will have more characters to identify with, potential-ly increasing positive identity growth (from positive characters, of course). Further, for individuals without a disability more representation may allow for the mere exposure effect and a reduction of stigmatization of individuals with disabilities.

The bad—changes aren't keeping up with society. There is still a large discrepancy between the highest reported percentage of disability within fic-tional media (11%) and the U.S. Census (19%). When it comes to learning about and understanding disability, knowledge is gained through exposure and accurate portrayals. Several studies examine how knowledge becomes a part of what we learn and how this knowledge can transform into our daily schemas and scripts (see Harris, 2009 for examples). With so few characters portraying a variety of disabilities it would be very difficult for viewers to gain knowledge about any one issue. Therefore, it would be difficult for accurate, complete information about a disability to become a part of a view-er's daily schema. This in turn *may* allow the limited portrayals to have a more powerful impact on viewers. For instance, Gerbner and associates (2002) might argue that if someone is not represented on television, not only do they not exist in the eyes of many individuals, but when encountering someone with a disability the "cultivated" individual will not know how to react, leading to possible marginalization of individuals. The few programs in which title characters have a disability (e.g., *Speechless*) may promote better understanding of that one particular disability to a small segment of viewers but overall disability underrepresentation is not likely to make a significant contribution to disability knowledge.

The ugly—the media always need a scapegoat. The crime drama always needs a killer, the sitcom someone to ridicule, the newspaper, a controversial angle to weigh in on. Sometimes individuals with disabilities are the easiest targets. Why not choose an obscure or abstract disability as the reason for criminal behavior? It adds an element of intrigue not found in the normal murder. Scholars have known and reported on what the media has been portraying (or not portraying) for over 70 years and there has been very little change. The impact of portrayals is potentially increased with image echoes and exposures across platforms, but this is an area of little study or discussion. Right now, today, individuals with disabilities are being exposed to either no or negative representations of the same disability and they ARE being negatively affected. A movie that came out 10 years ago, (*Gattaca*) showed an individual killing himself simply because he would rather be dead than live life in a wheelchair. There was nary a blip on the nation's radar about what that might say to viewers. But if that same individual was killing himself versus living with his race or gender, it may have created an uproar.

The media has the power to shape and facilitate lives and societies; at the very least the images it portrays should not harm either. The under- and misrepresentations of disabilities in the media is problematic and potentially harmful. Continuing research into disability portrayals and their potential effects may help individuals and organizations working to improve Hollywood's representation of disability and the lives of those affected by it.

As for the pithy—when I was young (maybe 10–12) I was in an amusement park with my family. I was walking with my older brother (who has cognitive disabilities) and some nearby kids started making fun of him. I don't know that he heard, but I did. My thought at the time was that they didn't even know him, so how could they make fun of him? What did they know about him or his disability? My thought later was guilt that I didn't speak up on his behalf or challenge the kids to explain themselves in some way, just stick up for my brother. This isn't to say that individuals with disabilities can't fight their own fights. It is simply to say, when we have the opportunity as a society to tell others that something may be wrong—a perception, an attitude, or behavior—we should take that opportunity. Maybe more appropriately, this text should end as it began, with a quote, but this one a little more positive from RJ Mitte. When asked by *The Daily Texan* why he thinks disability representation is important, he said:

> One of the biggest things [we work on] today is changing the mindset. It will affect our future, how people behave and what they do and how they talk to other people in the long run, especially when it comes down to disability,

because disability does not discriminate. It does not care what color you are, where you're from, who you are or what you do. Everyone is affected in one aspect or another. If you have inaccurate media [representation] about disability, it affects how people think about who they are. If you have media that, instead, depicts disability accurately, that shows people that disability is normal, that it can unite us as a whole under the human condition. Media needs to be a really positive thing. It needs to be honest because it affects people not just our age, but children. It has an impact on how children will grow up to treat each other and their own children. It even influences how parents treat their own children. You can give people brighter futures by having better disability representation. (Kallus 2015)

NOTES

1. Blair Underwood did hire a consultant in a wheelchair to help him in learning about spinal cord injuries and for some of the scripted content for the program *Ironside*.

2. Various outlets will argue between "impression" and "mocking" but regardless of intention, the message the public is seeing is what is important.

3. For more in this area I recommend the 2008 book *Entertainment-Education and Social Change: History, Research, and Practice* by Arvind Singhal, Michael Cody, Everett Rogers, and Miguel Sabido.

4. It is interesting that people that spend every day with individuals with cognitive disabilities still struggle with understanding the daily life of an individual with cognitive disability yet some media producers and policy makers think they "know what's best."

5. Suggesting or promoting boycotting programs with inaccurate portrayals is challenging in this instance. If one can turn off the television with a way to say to producers, "I love that the character has the disability but the portrayal is inaccurate—stereotyping, stigmatizing, etc.," then low ratings may promote change. BUT, because there are so few instances of disability in the media, "turning off" the program may be seen as a desire not to see the disability on television at all.

Bibliography

AAPD. 2017. Accessed April 12. www.aapd.com.

Abelman, Robert and David Atkin. 2000. "What children watch when they watch TV: Putting theory into practice." *Journal of Broadcasting & Electronic Media*, 44 (1), 143–154.

ADA Knowledge. 2017. "Guidelines for Reporting and Writing on People with Disabilities." Accessed April 12.http://adagreatlakes.com/Resources/Default.asp?category=16.

ADA Legacy Project. 2017. "Media Images and Portrayal Issues." Accessed April 24, 2017, http://www.adalegacy.com/media-images-and-portrayals-issue.

Ajzen, Isaac and Martin Fishbein. 1980. *Understanding attitudes and predicting social behavior*. Englewood Cliffs, NJ: Prentice Hall.

Ams Vans. 2017. "Wheelchair Barbie Dolls Were Not So Accessible." Accessed April 3, 2017. http://blog.amsvans.com/wheelchair-barbie-dolls-were-not-so-accessible/

Anderson, Tre'vell. 2016. "Disabled actors plead for a chance." *Los Angeles Times*, November 3. Sec. E

Andrews, Nigel. 1994. "Glamourised Gormlessness." *The Financial Times*, October 6.

Anti-Defamation League. 2017. "A Brief History of the Disability Rights Movement." Accessed April 6. https://www.adl.org/education/resources/backgrounders/disability-rights-movement

Attenhofer, Nancy A. 1969. "Teach them how to live." *Occupational Health Nursing*, 17 (10): 18–21.

Baker, William. 1999. "When can affective conditioning and mere exposure directly influence brand choice?" *Journal of Advertising*, 28 (4): 31–46.

Bamey, Chuck. 2012. "'Switched at Birth' shines the spotlight on deaf community." *Pittsburgh Post-Gazette*, January 5, Sec. Arts & Entertainment, A-12.

Bandura, Albert. 1986. *Social foundation of thought and action: A social cognitive theory*.Englewood Cliffs: NJ: Prentice-Hall.

———. 2001. "Social Cognitive Theory of Mass Communication." *Media Psychology*, 3, 265–299.

Barnes, Colin. 1991. "Discrimination: Disabled People and the Media." *Contact*, 70, 45–48.

Basil, Michael. 1996. "Identification as a mediator of celebrity effects." *Journal of Broadcasting & Electronic Media*, 40 (4), 478–495.

Bat-Chava, Yael. 2000. "Diversity of Deaf Identities." *American Annals of the Deaf*, 145 (5), 420–428.

Baughman, James. 2017. "Television comes to America 1947–1957." Accessed April 6.http://www.lib.niu.edu/1993/ihy930341.html.

Bauman, H-Dirksen. 2004. "Audism: Exploring the metaphysics of oppression." *Journal of Deaf Studies and Deaf Education*, 9, 2, 239–246.

..

110   *Bibliography*

Berger, Peter and Luckmann, Thomas. 1966. *The Social Construction of Reality: A Treatise in the Sociology of Knowledge.* New York, NY: Random House.

Blackwell, Debra, Jacqueline Lucas, and Tainya Clark. 2014. "Summary health statistics for U.S. adults: National health interview survey, 2012." *Vital and Health Statistics,* 10 (260).

Blase, Betty and Paula Kerr. 2000. "Intrapersonal and Interpersonal Health Education." *Journal of the American Dietetic Association,* 100 (4).

Blumler, Jay. 1969. "'Producers' attitudes towards television coverage of an election campaign: A case study." In *The Sociology of Mass Media Communicators,* edited by Paul Halmos, Keele: University of Keele.

Bogart, Kathleen. 2014. "The Role of Disability Self-Concept in Adaptation to Congenital or Acquired Disability." *Rehabilitation Psychology,* 59 (1), 107–115.

Bond, Bradley. 2008. "The Invisible Minority: Portrayals of Physical Disability on Children's Television Programming." *Conference Papers—National Communication Association.*

Bornstein, Robert F., and Paul R. D'Agostino. 1994. "The Attribution And Discounting Of Perceptual Fluency: Preliminary Tests Of A Perceptual Fluency/Attributional Model Of The Mere Exposure Effect." *Social Cognition* 12 (2): 103–128. doi:10.1521/soco.1994.12.2.103.

Bresnahan, Mary, Kami Silk, and Jie Zhaung. 2009. "You did this to yourself! Stigma and blame in lung cancer." A paper presented at the annual meeting of the National Communication Association.

Bronson, Jennifer, Laura Maruschak, and Marcus Berzofsky. (2015). "Disabilities among prison and jail inmates, 2011–12." *U.S. Department of Justice Bureau of Justice Statistics.* https://www.bjs.gov/content/pub/pdf/dpji1112.pdf. Accessed August 10, 2017.

Bryant, Jennings. 1990. *Television and the American Family.* Hillsdale, New Jersey: Lawrence Erlbaum Associates.

Burch, Susan and Ian Sutherland. (2006). "Who's Not Here Yet? American Disability History." *Radical History Review,* 92, 127–147.

Burningham, Kate and Geoff Cooper. 1999. "Being constructive: Social constructionism and the environment." *Sociology,* 33 (2): 297–299.

Burroughs, Virgina. 2006. "Disability hasn't slowed success of Marcus A. York: Former area resident lands guest role in 'The Office.'" *Dayton Daily News.* January 8, Life, E3.

Byrd, Keith. 1988. "Theory Regarding Attitudes and How They May Relate to Media Portrayals of Disability." *Journal of Applied Rehabilitation Counseling,* 20 (4): 36–38.

Byrd, Keith, Timothy Elliott, Randall McDaniel, and Robert Rhoden. 1980. "Television programming and disability: A ten-year span. *International Journal of Rehabilitation Research* 3 (3): 321–326.

Canwest News Service. 2010. "Lynch revels in her role as series' version of Cruella de Vil." *Edmonton Journal,* April 12, Sec. A&E, B1.

Carter, Michael and Danielle Mireles. 2016a. "Exploring the Relationship Between Deaf Identity Verification Processes and Self-Esteem." *Identity: An International Journal of Theory and Research,* 16, 2, 102–114.

———. 2016b. "New Directions in Identity Theory and Research." In *New Directions in Identity Theory and Research,* edited by Jan Stets and Richard Serpe. UK: Oxford Publishing, 509–538.

Caton, Sue and Melanie Chapman. 2016. "The Use of Social Media and People with Intellectual Disability: A Systematic Review and Thematic Analysis." *Journal of Intellectual & Developmental Disability,* 41 (2), 125–139.

Charmaz, Kathy. 1998a. "The body, identity, and self: Adapting to impairment." In *Health, illness, and healing,* edited by Kathy Charmaz and Debora Paterniti, 95–112. Los Angeles: Roxbury.

———. 1998b. "'Discoveries' of self in illness." In *Health, illness, and healing,* edited by Kathy Charmaz and Debora Paterniti, 72–82. Los Angeles: Roxbury.

Chen, Ling, Guangchao Feng, and Vivienne Leung. 2014. "Sources, contents, and students' social learning about persons with a disability." *Chinese Journal of Communication,* 7 (4): 429–445. doi:10.1080/17544750.2014.945603.

Cheng, Mei-Hua, Yi-Chen Wu, and Ming-Chih Chen. 2016. "Television Meets Facebook: The Correlation between TV Ratings and Social Media." *American Journal of Industrial and Business Management*, 6, 282–290.

Clark, Cedric. 1969. "Spring Television and social control: Some observations on the portrayals of ethnic minorities." *Television Quarterly*, Spring, 18–22.

Clogston, John. 1990. *Disability Coverage in 16 Newspapers*. Louisville: Advocado Press.

Codd, Judy. 1966. "The Effects of Television on Mentally Handicapped Children." *The Speech Teacher*, 15 (4): 328–331.

Cohen, Jonathan. 2001. "Defining Identification: A Theoretical Look at the Identification of Audiences with Media Characters." *Mass Communication and Society* 4 (3): 245–64. doi:10.1207/s15327825mcs0403_01.

Cole, Charlotte, Cairo Arafat, Chava Tidhar, Wafa Tafesh, and Nathan Fox. 2003. "The educational impact of *Rechov Sumsum/Shara'a Simsim*: A *Sesame Street* television series to promote respect and understanding among children living in Israel, West Bank, and Gaza." *International Journal of Behavioral Development*, 27, 409–432.

Collins, Leah and Miranda Furtado. 2011. "From Uncle Buck to Dr. Evil: The movies' top moronic siblings." *Vancouver Sun*, August 26.

CTV News. 2013. "'Switched at Birth' airs silent episode to highlight deaf perspective." March 1, Accessed April 6, 2017. http://ctv.news/CfRaRud

Cumberbatch, Guy, and Ralph M. Negrine. 1992. *Images of disability on television*. London: Routledge.

Dahl, Marilyn. 1993. "Role of the Media in Promoting Images of Disability—Disability as Metaphor: The Evil Crip." *Canadian Journal Of Communication*, 18(1), 75–80.

Davison, W. Phillips. 1983. "The Third-Person Effect in Communication." *Public Opinion Quarterly*, 47 (1), 1–15. DOI: 10.1086/268763.

DeLeire, Thomas. 2000. "The Unintended Consequences of the Americans with Disabilities Act." *Regulation*, 23 (1), 21–24.

Diamond, Karen E., and Katherine R. Kensinger. 2002. "Vignettes from Sesame Street: Preschooler's Ideas about Children with Down Syndrome and Physical Disability." *Early Education & Development* 13 (4): 409–22. doi:10.1207/s15566935eed1304_5.

Dibble, Jayson, Tilo Hartmann, and Sarah Rosaen. 2016. "Parasocial Interaction and Parasocial Relationships: Conceptual Clarification and a Critical Assessment of Measures." *Human Communication Research*, 42, 21–44.

Diefenbach, Donald. 1997. "The Portrayal of Mental Illness on Primetime Television." *Journal of Community Psychology*, 25 (3): 289–302.

Diefenbach, Donald and Mark D. West. 2007. "Television and attitudes toward mental health issues: Cultivation analysis and the third-Person effect." *Journal of Community Psychology* 35 (2): 181–95. doi:10.1002/jcop.20142.

Dillon, Carol, Keith Byrd, and Dianne Byrd. 1980. "Television and disability." *Journal of Rehabilitation*, 46 (4), 67–69.

"Disabilities." 2017. *World Health Organization*. World Health Organization. Accessed April 3. http://www.who.int/topics/disabilities/en/.

"Disability Language Guide." 2017. http://ncdj.org/style-guide. Accessed April 12.

Doering, Katie. December 12, 2009. "Glee teaching life lessons about abilities: For the first time, students with exceptionalities are being included in mainstream TV." *The Hamilton Spectator*, Weekend Reader, WR09.

Donaldson, Joy. 1981. "The Visibility and Image of Handicapped People on Television." *Exceptional Children* 47 (6): 413–16. doi:10.1177/001440298104700602.

Donnelly, Colleen. 2016. "Re-visioning Negative Archetypes of Disability and Deformity in Fantasy: Wicked, Maleficent, and Game of Thrones." *Disability Studies Quarterly*, 36(4).

Duff, Brittany R. L. and Ronald J. Faber. 2011. "Missing the Mark: Advertising Avoidance and Distractor Devaluation." *Journal of Advertising*, 40 (2): 51–62.

Dunn, Dana and Erin Andrews. 2015. "Person-first and identity-first language: Developing psychologists' cultural competence using disability language." *American Psychologist*, 70 (3), 255–264, http://dx.doi.org/10.1037/a0038636.

Dutta-Bergman, Mohan J. 2004. "Primary Sources of Health Information: Comparisons in the Domain of Health Attitudes, Health Cognitions, and Health Behaviors." *Health Communication* 16 (3): 273–88. doi:10.1207/s15327027hc1603_1.

Elliott, Timothy, and Keith Byrd. 1983. Attitude change toward disability through television portrayal. *Journal of Applied Rehabilitation Counseling*, 14 (2) 35–37.

Ellis, Kathleen. 2003. "Reinforcing the stigma: The representation of disability in *Gattaca*." *Australian Screen Education*, 31, 111–114.

Ellis, Kathleen and Mike Kent. 2016. *Disability and Social Media: Global Perspectives*. New York: Routledge.

Englandkennedy, Elizabeth. 2008. "Media Representations of Attention Deficit Disorder: Portrayals of Cultural Skepticism in Popular Media." *The Journal of Popular Culture* 41 (1): 91–117. doi:10.1111/j.1540–5931.2008.00494.x.

Eyal, Keren and Alan Rubin. 2003. "Viewer Aggression and Homophily, Identification, and Parasocial Relationships with Television Characters." *Journal of Broadcasting & Electronic Media*, 47 (1), 77–98.

Farnall, Olan, and Kim A. Smith. 1999. "Reactions to People with Disabilities: Personal Contact versus Viewing of Specific Media Portrayals." *Journalism & Mass Communication Quarterly* 76 (4): 659–72. doi:10.1177/107769909907600404.

FCC. 2017. "21st Century Communications and Video Accessibility Act (CVAA)." Accessed April 24, 2017. https://www.fcc.gov/consumers/guides/21st-century-communications-and-video-accessibility-act-cvaa.

Ferrara, Kate, Jan Burns, and Hayley Mills. 2015. "Public Attitudes Toward People With Intellectual Disabilities After Viewing Olympic or Paralympic Performance." *Adapted Physical Activity Quarterly* 32 (1): 19–33.

Ferré, John. 2009. "A Short History of Media Ethics in the United States." In *Mass Media Ethics*, edited by L. Wilkins and C. Christians. New York: Taylor and Francis, 15–27.

Fishbein, Martin and Isaac Ajzen. 1975. *Belief attitude, intention, and behavior: An introduction to theory and research*. Reading, MA: Addison-Wesley.

Foss, Katherine. 2009. "Gil Grissom and his hidden condition: Constructions of hearing loss and deafness in *CSI: Crime Scene Investigation*." *Disability Studies Quarterly*, 29 (2).

———. 2014a. "(De)Stigmatizing the Silent Epidemic: Representations of Hearing Loss in Entertainment Television." *Health Communication*, 29 (9): 888–900. DOI: 10.1080/10410236.2013.814079.

———. 2014b. "Constructing Hearing Loss or 'Deaf Gain?' Voice, Agency, and Identity in Television's Representation of d/Deafness." *Critical Studies in Media Communication*, 31:5, 426–447, DOI: 10.1080/15295036.2014.968603

Fruth, Laurel and Allan Padderud. 1985. "Portrayals of Mental Illness in Daytime Television Serials." *Journalism Quarterly*, 62 (2), 384–387.

Fujioka, Yuki. 1999. "Television portrayals and African-American stereotypes: Examination of television effects when direct contact is lacking." *Journalism and Mass Communication Quarterly*, 76 (1): 52–75.

Gagliardi, Katy. 2017. "Facebook Captions: Kindness, or Inspiration Porn?" *M/C Journal* 20 (3), 1.

Gambone, Michael D. 2005. *Williams-Ford TAMU Military History: Greatest Generation Comes Home: The Veteran in American Society*. College Station, US: Texas A&M University Press.

Ganahl, Dennis and Mark Arbuckle. 2001. "Primetime Portrayal of Persons with Disabilities: A Study of Representation, Stereotype, and Impact." A paper presented at the annual meeting of the Association for Education in Journalism and Mass Communication.

Gardner, James M., and Michael S. Radel. 1978. "Portrait of The Disabled In The Media." *Journal Of Community Psychology* 6 (3): 269–274. doi:10.1002/1520–6629.

Genzlinger, Neil. 2013. "Disabled but still dangerous 'Ironside,' the Series Remake, Has Its Debut on NBC." *New York Times*, October 2, C2.

Gerbner, George. 1959. "Mental Illness on Television: A Study of Censorship." *Journal of Broadcasting*, 4 (3): 293–303.

Gerbner, George, and P. H. Tannenbaum. 1960. "Regulation of Mental Illness Content In Motion Pictures and Television." *International Communication Gazette* 6 (4): 365–385. doi:10.1177/001654926000600403.

Gerbner, George, Larry Gross, Michael Morgan, Nancy Signorielli. 1994. "Growing up with television: The cultivation perspective." In *Media Effects: Advances in theory and research*, edited by Jennings Bryand and Dolf Zillman, 17–42. Hillsdale, NJ: Lawrence Erlbaum Associates, Inc.

Gerbner, George, Larry Gross, Michael Morgan, Nancy Signorielli, and James Shanahan. 2002. "Growing up with television: Cultivation processes." In *Media Effects: Advances in theory and research (2 nd Edition)*, edited by Jennings Bryant and Dolf Zillman, 43–68. Hillsdale, NJ: Lawrence Erlbaum Associates, Inc.

Gill, James, Sanford Grossbart, and Russell Laczniak. 1988. "Influence of involvement, commitment and familiarity on brand beliefs and attitudes of viewers exposed to alternative ad claim strategies." *Journal of Advertising*, 17 (2): 33–43.

Gill, Liz. 1992. "Shaking off the image handicap." *The Times,* June 9, Features.

Gillmore, Mary, Matthew Archibald, Diane Morrison, and Anthony Wilsdon, et al. 2002. "Teen sexual behavior: Applicability of the theory of reasoned action." *Journal of Marriage and Family*, 64, 4, 885–897.

Glauberman, Nancy. 1980. "The influence of positive TV portrayals on children's behavior and attitude toward the physically disabled." Unpublished doctoral dissertation at Columbia University, New York, NY.

Golos, Debbie. 2010. "The Representation of Deaf Characters in Children's Educational Television in the US." *Journal of Children and Media*, 4 (3), 248–264.

Greiwe, Elizabeth. 2016. "Flashback: How an 'ugly law' stayed on Chicago's books for 93 years." *Chicago Tribune*, June 23, Accessed April 12. http://www.chicagotribune.com/news/opinion/commentary/ct-ugly-laws-disabilities-chicago-history-flashback-perspec-0626-md-20160622-story.html

Grodin, Debra and Thomas Lindlof. 1996. *Constructing the Self in a Mediated World*. California: Sage Publications.

Gunderman, Dan. 2017. "Revisiting the atrocities that once consumed the halls of Willowbrook State School in Staten Island." *Daily News*, April 9, Accessed April 24, 2017. http://www.nydailynews.com/news/national/atrocities-consumed-halls-willowbrook-school-article-1.3030716.

Hall, Heather and Patricia Minnes. 1999. "Attitudes Toward *Persons* with Down Syndrome: The Impact of Television." *Journal of Developmental and Physical Disabilities*, 11 (1), 61–76.

Haller, Beth. 1995. "Rethinking Models of Media Representation of Disability." *Disability Studies Quarterly*, 15 (2), 26–30.

———. 2010. *Representing disability in an ableist world: Essays on mass media*. Louisville: Advocado Press.

Haller, Beth and Lingling Zhang. 2013. "Stigma or empowerment? What do disabled people say about their representation in news and entertainment media?" *Review of Disability Studies*, 9 (4): 19–33.

Haller, Beth, Bruce Dorries, and Jessica Rahn. 2006. "Media labeling versus the US disability community identity: a study of shifting cultural language." *Disability & Society*, 21 (1): 61–75, DOI: 10.1080/09687590500375416.

Hardin, M., and B. Hardin, B. 2004. The "supercrip" in sport media: Wheelchair athletes discuss hegemony's disabled hero. *Sociology of Sport Online,* 7 (1). http://physed.otago.ac.nz/sosol/v7i1/v7il_1.html.

Harrell, Erika. 2015. "Crime Against Persons with Disabilities, 2009–2013." *U.S. Department of Justice Bureau of Justice Statistics*. https://www.bjs.gov/content/pub/pdf/capd0913st.pdf. Accessed August 10, 2017.

Harris, Richard J. 1999. *A Cognitive Psychology of Mass Communication*. Mahwah, NJ: Lawrence Erlbaum Associates.

Harwood, Jake. 1999. "Age identification, social identity gratifications, and television view-ing." *Journal of Broadcasting & Electronic Media* 43 (1): 123–36. doi:10.1080/08838159909364479.

Hayakawa, S.I. and Alan Hayakawa. 1993. "The Empty Eye." *ETC: A Review of General Semantics*, 137–155.

Hayer, Melissa. 2011. "Katie LeClerc portrays girl with hearing loss on ABC Family." *The Oklahoman*, July 4, Sec. Life, 1C.

Head, Sydney W. 1954. "Content Analysis of Television Drama Programs." *The Quarterly of Film Radio and Television* 9 (2): 175–94. doi:10.2307/1209974.

Heeter, Carrie, H. Perlstadt, and Bradley Greenberg. 1984. "Health incidence, stages of illness and treatment on popular television programs." A paper presented at the annual meeting of the International Communication Association.

Hemsley, Bronwyn and Stephen Dann. 2014. "Social media and social marketing in relation to facilitated communication: Harnessing the affordances of social media for knowledge trans-lation." *Evidence-Based Communication Assessment and Intervention*, 8 (4), 187–206.

Herzog, Herta. 1944. "What do we really know about daytime serial listeners." In *Radio Research*, edited by Paul Lazarsfeld and Frank Stanton, 2–23, London: Sage.

Holloway, Daniel. 2010. "GLAAD: Only 6 disabled primetime chracters." *The Hollywood Reporter*, October 6, Accessed April 12, 2017, http://www.hollywoodreporter.com/news/glaad-only-6-disabled-primetime-28835.

Holton, Avery. E. 2013. "What's Wrong With Max? Parenthood and the Portrayal of Autism Spectrum Disorders." *Journal of Communication Inquiry* 37 (1): 45–63. doi:10.1177/0196859912472507.

Holton, Avery. E., Laura C. Farrell, and Julie L. Fudge. 2014. "A Threatening Space?: Stigma-tization And The Framing Of Autism In The News." *Communication Studies* 65 (2): 189–207. doi:10.1080/10510974.2013.855642.

Hu, Yifeng. 2015. "Health communication research in the digital age: A systematic review." *Journal of Communication In Healthcare* 8, no. 4: 260–288.

Huesmann, L. Rowell and Laramie Taylor. 2006. "The Role of Media Violence in Violent Behavior." *Annual Review of Public Health*, 27, 393–415.

Igartua, Juan-Jose' and Jair Vega Casnova. 2016. "Identification with Characters, Elaboration, and Counterarguing in Entertainment-Education Interventions through Audiovisual Fic-tion." *Journal of Health Communication*, 21 (3), 293–300, DOI:10.1080/10810730.2015.1064494.

Itzkoff, Dave. 2010. "'Family Guy,' Palin and the Limits of Laughter." *New York Times*, February 19, Accessed April 12. http://www.nytimes.com/2010/02/20/arts/television/20family.html?scp=1sq=22seth20macfarlane22;st=cse.

Kallus, Megan. February 20, 2015. "Q&A: 'Breaking Bad' star RJ Mitte discusses Walter White, cerebral palsy, and working with disability." *The Daily Texan*, http://www.dailytexanonline.com/2015/02/20/qa-breaking-bad-star-rj-mitte-discusses-walter-white-cerebral-palsy-and-working-with, Accessed August 10, 2017.

Kama, Amit. 2004. "Supercrips versus the pitiful handicapped: Reception of disabling images by disabled audience members." *Communications* 29 (4). doi:10.1515/comm.2004.29.4.447.

Kamins, Michael, Meribeth Brand, Stuart Hoeke, and John Moe. 1989. "Two-sided versus One-sided Celebrity Endorsements: The Impact on Advertising Effectiveness and Credibil-ity." *Journal of Advertising*, 18 (2), 4–10.

Katz, Elihu. 1980. "On Conceptualizing Media Effects." *Studies in Communications*, 1, 119–141.

Kavoori, Anandam. 1999. "Discursive texts, reflexive audiences: Global trends in television news texts and audience reception." *Journal of Broadcasting & Electronic Media*, 43 (3), 386–395.

Kelly, Michael. 2001. "Disability and Community." In *Handbook of Disability Studies*, edited by Gary Albrecht, Katherine Seelman, and Michael Bury, 396–411, Thousand Oaks, CA: Sage Publications.

Kennedy, Greg. 2012. "The disabled acting community works to end of decades of 'invisibil-ity.'" *The National*, November 19.

Kim, Ki Joon and Shyam Sundar. 2016. "Mobile Persuasion: Can Screen Size and Presentation Mode Make a Difference to Trust." *Human Communication Research*, 42, 45–70.

Kincheloe, Pam. 2010. "Do androids dream of electric speech? The construction of cochlear implant identity on American television and the 'New Deaf Cyborg.'" *Media & Culture*, 13 (3).

Kitzinger, Jenny. 1999. "A sociology of media power: Key issues in audience reception research." In *Message Received*, edited by Greg Philo, 3–20, New York: Addison-Wesley Longman.

Klobas, Lauri E. 1988. *Disability drama in television and film*. Jefferson: McFarland.

Ladd, Paddy. 2003. *Understanding Deaf Culture: In Search of Deafhood*. Multilingual Matters.

Longmore, Paul. 1987. *Why I Burned My Book: And Other Essays on Disability*. Philadelphia: Temple University Press.

Lupton, Deborah. 1994. *Medicine as Culture: Illness, Disease and the Body in Western Societies*. London: Sage Publications.

Mares, Marie-Louise and Emily Acosta. 2008. "Be Kind to Three-Legged Dogs: Children's Literal Interpretations of TV's Moral Lessons." *Media Psychology*, 11, 377–399.

Mastersons, Lawrie. 2010. "The blind leading the blonde?" *Sunday Herald Sun*, October 24, Sec. TVGuide, 3.

Maudlin, Julie. 2007. "Life goes on: Disability, Curriculum and Popular Culture." In *Curriculum and the Cultural Body*, edited by Stephanie Springgay and Debra Freeman, 113–129, New York: Peter Lang.

Matias, Nicole and Maria Sousa. 2017. "Mobile Health, a Key Factor Enhancing Disease Prevention Campaigns: Looking for Evidences in Kidney Disease Prevention." *Journal of Information Systems Engineering & Management*, 2 (1), doi:http://dx.doi.org/10.20897/jisem.201703.

McQuail, Denis. 1994. *Mass communication theory: an introduction*. London: Sage Publ.

Miller, Gerri. 2016. "Cool Jobs: Keeping TV science honest" *Science News for Students*, September 8, Accessed April 20, 2017. https://www.sciencenewsforstudents.org/article/cool-jobs-keeping-tv-science-honest.

Miller, David and Greg Philo. 1999. "The effective media." In *Message Received*, edited by Greg Philo, 21–32, New York: Addison-Wesley Longman.

Minnesota Department of Administration Council on Developmental Disabilities. 2013. "Willowbrook Leads to New Protections of Rights." Accessed April 12, 2017. http://mn.gov/mnddc/ada-legacy/ada-legacy-moment9.html.

Moe, Peter. 2012. "Revealing Rather than Concealing Disability: The Rhetoric of Parkinson's Advocate Michael J. Fox." *Rhetoric Review*, 31 (4), 443–460. DOI:10.1080/07350198.2012.711200.

Moy, Patricia, and Michael Pfau. 2000. *With malice toward all?: The media and public confidence in democratic institutions*. Westport, CT: Praeger.

Moyer-Guse,' Emily. 2008. "Toward a Theory of Entertainment Persuasion: Explaining the Persuasive Effects of Entertainment-Education Messages." *Communication Theory*, 18 (3), 407–425.

Murphy, Robert.1998. "The damaged self." In *Understanding and Applying Medical Anthropology*. Edited by Peter Brown, California: Mayfield Publishing, 322–333.

National Organization on Disability. 2017. "About." Accessed April 12. www.nod.org.

Navarro, Mireya. May 13, 2007. "Clearly, Frankly, Unabashedly Disabled." *New York Times*, Sec. 9, 1.

Nelson, Jack. 1994. *The Disabled, the Media and the Information Age*. Westport, CT: Greenwood Press.

Nelson, Jack. 2000. "The Media Role in Building the Disability Community." *Journal of Mass Media Ethics*, 15 (3), 180–193.

Nelson, Jacob and James Webster. 2016. "Audience Currencies in the Age of Big Data." *International Journal on Media Management*, 18 (1), 9–24.

Nielsen Total Audience Report Q4. 2016. Accessed April 24, 2017, http://www.nielsen.com/content/dam/corporate/us/en/reports-downloads/2017-reports/total-audience-report-q4-2016.pdf.

Ninan, Reena. 2016. "'Finding Dory' Shatters Stereotypes About Disabilities." *CBS* News, June 21. http://www.cbsnews.com/news/finding-dory-shatters-stereotypes-about-disabilities-with-empowering-characters/.

Nordhielm, Christie. 2002. "The influence of Level of Process on Advertising Repetition Effects." *Journal of Consumer Research*, 29 (3): 371–382. doi: 10.1086/344428.

Nunnally, Jum. 1957. "The Communication of Mental Health Information: A Comparison of the Opinions of Experts and the Public with Mass Media Presentations." *Behavioral Science*, 2 (3), 222–230.

Olney, Marjorie and Amanda Kim. 2001. "Beyond Adjustment: Integration of cognitive disability into identity." *Disability & Society*, 16 (4), 563–583.

Owen, Rob. 2013 "A silent show for 'Switched at Birth.'" *Pittsburgh Post-Gazette*, March 1, Sec. Arts & Entertainment, B-1.

Padden, Carol and Tom Humphries. 2005. *Inside Deaf Culture*. Cambridge, MA: Harvard University Press.

Park, Justin, Jason Faulkner, and Mark Schaller. 2003. "Evolved Disease-Avoidance Processes and Contemporary Anti-Social Behavior: Prejudicial Attitudes and Avoidance of People with Physical Disabilities." *Journal of Nonverbal Behavior*, 27 (2), 65–87.

Pearl, Rebecca, Rebecca Puhl, and Kelly Brownell. 2012. "Positive Media Portrayals of Obese Persons: Impact on Attitudes and Image Preferences." *Health Psychology*, 31 (6), 821–9. DOI: 10.103\/a0027189.

Pearson, David. 1993. "Post-mass culture." *Society*, 30 (5), 17–22.

Pemberton, Kim. 2013. "Glee actress inspires young fans who have Down syndrome; Lauren Potter plays cheerleader on popular TV series." *The Vancouver Sun*, May 24, Sec. West-Coast News, A7.

Perry, Jonathan. 2004. "Interviewing people with intellectual disabilities." In *International Handbook of Applied Research in Intellectual Disabilities*, edited by Eric Emerson, Chris Hatton, Travis Thompson, and Trevor Parmenter, 115–131, Hoboken, NJ: John Wiley & Sons.

Peterson, Jillian. April 21, 2014. "Mental Illness Not Usually Linked to Crime, Research Finds." American Psychological Association. http://www.apa.org/news/press/releases/2014/04/mental-illness-crime.aspx. Accessed August 10, 2017.

Petty, Richard and John Cacioppo. 1986. "The Elaboration Likelihood Model of Persuasion." *Advances in Experimental Social Psychology*, 19, 123–205.

Purdy, Joscelyn. 1989. "Disability doesn't hinder their acting careers A young girl who lost a leg is featured in a TV series, another youngster in a wheelchair acts in a Christmas commercial." *The Toronto Star*, December 17, Sec. People, D5.

Quinlan, Margaret and Benjamin Bates. 2008. "Dances and Discourses of (Dis)Ability: Heather Mills's Embodiment of Disability on *Dancing with the Stars.*" *Text and Performance Quarterly*, 28 (1–2), 64–80.

———. 2010. "Are our president learning? Unpacking the enthymematic connections in the speech mistakes of President George W. Bush." *Journal of Research in Special Educational Needs*, 10 (1), 3–12, doi: 10.1111=j.1471–3802.2009.01132.x.

Quintero Johnson, Jessie, Kristen Harrison, and Brian Quick. 2013. "Understanding the Effectiveness of the Entertainment-Education Strategy: An Investigation of how Audience Involvement, Message Processing, and Message Design Influence Health Information Recall." *Journal of Health Communication*, 18 (2), 160–178.

Raynor, Olivia, and Katherine Hayward. 2008. "Performers with Disabilities in Film and TV: What the Screen Actors Guild Data Show." Paper presented at the annual meeting for the National Communication Association, San Diego, CA.

Rea, Steven. 1994. "In 'Forrest Gump,' village idiot's tour of U.S. milestones." *The Philadelphia Inquirer*, July 6, Sec. Entertainment, E01.

Redeafined. 2013. "'Switched at Birth's' First Big Mistake: An Inaccurate Representation of Cochlear Implants." Accessed April 13, 2017 - http://www.redeafined.com/2013/07/switched-at-births-first-big-mistake.html.

"Rehabilitation Act of 1973." 2017. Accessed April 12. https://www.eeoc.gov/eeoc/history/50th/thelaw/rehab_act-1973.cfm.

Renwick, Rebecca. 2016. "Rarely Seen, Seldom Heard: People with Intellectual Disabilities in the Mass Media." In *Intellectual Disability and Stigma* edited by Katrina Scior and Shirli Werner. London: Palmgrave MacMillan.

Renwick, Rebecca, Ann Schormans, and Deborah Shore. 2014. "Hollywood takes on intellectual/development disability: Cinematic representations of occupational participation." *OTJR: Occupation, Participation and Health*, 34 (1), 20–31.

Research and Training Center on Independent Living by the Rocky Mountain Americans with Disabilities Association. 2013. "How to Write and Report about People with Disabilities." Accessed April 13, 2017,http://rtcil.drupal.ku.edu/sites/rtcil.drupal.ku.edu/files/images/galleries/Guidelines%208th%20edition.pdf.

Rigby, Jacob, Duncan Brumby, Anna Cox, Sandy Gould. 2016. "Watching Movies on Netflix: Investigating the Effect of Screen Size on Viewer Immersion." Mobile HCI'16 Proceedings of the 18th International Conference on Human-Computer Interaction with Mobile Devices and Services Adjunct, Florence, Italy, 714–721. DOI: 10.1145/2957265.2961843.

Riley, Charles. 2005. *Disability and the Media: Prescriptions for Change*. Hanover, NE: University Press of New England.

Roberts, E.J. 1982. "Television and sexual learning in childhood." In *Television and behavior: Ten years of scientific progress and implications for the eighties, Vol. II, technical reviews*, edited by David Pearl, L. Bouthilet, and J. Lazar. (DHHS Publication No. ADM 82–1196). Washington, DC: US Government Printing Office.

Roberts, Tomi-Ann and Jennifer Gettman. 2004. "Mere exposure: Gender differences in the negative effects of priming a state of self-objectification." *Sex Roles*, 51 (1–2): 17–27, DOI: 10.1023/B:SERS.0000032306.20462.22.

Rosenburg, Alyssa. 2013. "How Technical Advisors Help 'Parenthood' and 'Ironside' Get Autism and Spinal Cord Injury Right." *Think Progress*, July 29, Accessed April 24, 2017, https://thinkprogress.org/how-technical-advisors-help-parenthood-and-ironside-get-autism-and-spinal-cord-injuries-right-cc3144443870.

Ross, Karen. 1997. "But where's me in it? Disability, broadcasting and the audience." *Media, Culture & Society* 19 (4): 669–77. doi:10.1177/016344397019004009.

Ryan, Ellen, Selina Bajorek, Amanda Beaman, and Ann Anas. 2005. "I Just Want You to Know that 'Them' is Me: Intergroup Perspectives on Communication and Disability." In *Intergroup Communication: Multiple Perspectives*, edited by J. Harwood and H. Giles, 117–137. New York: Peter Lang.

Samsel, Maria and Prithvi Perepa. 2013. "The impact of media representation of disabilities on teachers' perceptions." *Support for Learning*, 28 (4), 138–145.

Schiappa, Edward, Peter Gregg, and Dean Hewes. 2005. "The Parasocial Contact Hypothesis." *Communication Monographs*, 72 (1), 92–115.

Schroeder, Jonathan E., and Detlev Zwick. 2004. "Mirrors of Masculinity: Representation and Identity in Advertising Images." *Consumption Markets & Culture* 7 (1): 21–52. doi:10.1080/1025386042000212383.

Seale, Clive. 2003. "Health and media: An overview." *Sociology of Health & Illness*, 25 (6), 513–531. DOI: 10.111/1467–9566.t01–1-00356.

Sharf, Barbara, Victoria Freimuth, P. Greenspon, and C. Plotnick. 1996. "Confronting cancer on *thirtysomething*: audience response to health content on entertainment television." *Journal of Health Communication*, 1 (2), 157–172.

Shpigelman, Carmit-Noa, and Carol J. Gill. 2014. "Facebook Use by Persons with Disabilities." *Journal of Computer-Mediated Communication* 19 (3), 610–624.

Shrum, L.J., Robert Wyer, Thomas O'Guinn. 1998. "The effects of television consumption on social perceptions: The use of priming procedures to investigate psychological processes. *Journal of Consumer Research*, 24 (4): 447–459.

Signorielli, Nancy. 1989. "The stigma of mental illness on television." *Journal of Broadcasting & Electronic Media* 33 (3): 325–31. doi:10.1080/08838158909364085.

———. 2009a. "Minority representation in prime time: 2000 to 2008." *Communication Research Reports*, 26(4): 323–336.

———. 2009b. "Race and sex in prime time: A look at occupations and occupational prestige." *Mass Communication and Society*, 12(3): 332–352.

———. 2016. "Sex and Race in Prime Time: Five Decades of Research." In *Race and Gender in Electronic Media: Content, Context, Culture*. Edited by Rebecca Lind, New York: Routledge.

Singer, Dorothy and Jerome Singer. 1998. "Developing Critical Viewing Skills and Media Literacy in Children." *The Annals of the American Academy of Political and Social Science*, 557 (1), 164–179, doi: 10.1177/0002716298557000013.

Singh, Karendeep, Kaitlin Drouin, Lisa Newmark, JaeHo Lee, Arild Faxvaag, Ronen Rozenblum, Erika Pabo, Adam Landman, Elissa Klinger and David Bates. 2016. "Many Mobile Health Apps Target High-Need, High-Cost Populations but Gaps Remain." *Health Affairs*, 25 (12), 2310–2318.

Smedema, Susan. 2014. "Core self-evaluations and well-being in persons with disabilities." *Rehabilitation Psychology*, 59 (4), 407–414.

Smith, Stacy, Amy Nathanson, and Barbara Wilson. 2002. "Part-time Television: Assessing Violence During the Most Popular Viewing Hours. *Journal of Communication*, 52 (1): 84–111. DOI: 10.1111/j.1460–2466.2002.tb02534.x

Smith, Frank, Geoffrey Trivax, David Zuehlke, Paul Lowinger, and Thieu Nghiem. 1972. "Health information during a week of television." *The New England Journal of Medicine*, 286 (10): 516–520. DOI: 10.1056/NEJM197203092861005.

Snyder, Sharon and David Mitchell. 2006. *Cultural Locations of Disability*. Chicago: University of Chicago Press.

Sobsey, Dick .1994. *Violence and abuse in the lives of people with disabilities*. Baltimore: Paul H. Brookes Publishing Co.

South Bend Tribune. 2004. "'Facts of Life' star to speak at Saint Mary's," February 4.

SPJ Code of Ethics. 2017. https://www.spj.org/ethicscode.asp. Accessed October 2, 2017.

Starck, Kenneth. 2001. "What's Right/Wrong with Journalism Ethics Research?" *Journalism Studies*, 2 (1): 133–150.

Starr, Michael. 2016. "Prime opportunity 'Speechless' star Micah Fowler's trailblazing role." *New York Post*, November 16, Sec. All Editions, 54.

———. 2017. "Kennish, anyone? 'Switched at Birth' family back after long hiatus." *New York Post*, January 31, Sec. All Editions, 58.

Strauss, Gary. 2008. "For teen star of 'Breaking Bad,' disability is no obstacle: RJ Mitte has cerebral palsy, and so does his character." *USA Today*, February 21, Sec. Life, 8D.

Strong, Deborah and William Brown. 2008. "Effects of a Children's Entertainment-Education Television Program in Nepal on Beliefs and Behavior toward People with Disabilities." A paper presented at the annual meeting of the National Communication Association, San Diego, CA.

Taylor, Wilson. 1957. "Gauging the Mental Health Content of the Mass Media." *Journalism and Mass Communication Quarterly* 34 (2): 191–201

The Arc. 2017. "History of the Arc." Accessed April 6.http://www.thearc.org/.

The Times & Transcript. 2014. "Making drama out of 'ordinary life' can be murder." November 13, Sec. Features, C3.

Thornton, JoAnn and Otto Wahl. 1996. "Impact of a newspaper article on attitudes toward mental illness." *Journal of Community Psychology*, 24 (1), 17–25. DOI: 10.1002/(SICI)1520–6629(199601)24:117::AID-JCOP23.0.CO;2–0.

Turner, Keith and Edna Szymanski. 1990. "Work adjustment of people with congenital disabilities: A longitudinal perspective from birth to adulthood." *Journal of Rehabilitation*, 56 (3), 19–24.

US Census Bureau Public Information Office. 2016. "Nearly 1 in 5 People Have a Disability in the U.S., Census Bureau Reports - Miscellaneous - Newsroom - U.S. Census Bureau." *Nearly 1 in 5 People Have a Disability in the U.S., Census Bureau Reports - Miscellaneous - Newsroom - U.S. Census Bureau.* May 19. https://www.census.gov/newsroom/releases/archives/miscellaneous/cb12–134.html.

Wahl, Otto and Rachel Roth. 1982. "Television images of mental illness: Results of a metropolitan Washington media watch." *Journal of Broadcasting*, 26(2): 599–605.

Wahl, Otto, Erin Hanrahan, Kelly Karl, Erin Lasher, and Janel Swaye. 2007. "The depiction of mental illnesses in children's television programs." *Journal of Community Psychology* 35 (1): 121–33. doi:10.1002/jcop.20138.

Walsh-Childers, Kim. 2016. *Mass Media and Health: Examining Media Impact on Individuals and the Health Environment*, New York: Taylor and Francis.

Webster, James. 1998. "The audience." *Journal of Broadcasting & Electronic Media*, 42 (2), 190–207.

Welch, Polly. 1994. *Strategies of Teaching Universal Design*. Boston, MA: AdaptiveEnvironments Center.

Westerman, David and Paul Skalski. 2010. "Computers and Telepresence: A Ghost in the Machine?" In *Immersed in Media: Telepresence in Everyday Life*, edited by C.C. Bracken and P. Skalski, 63–86. New York: Routledge.

Witkin, Stanley. 1999. "Constructing our future." *Social Work*, 44 (1): 5–8. Retrieved from: http://www.jstor.org/stable/23717887.

Woodburn, Danny and Jay Ruderman. 2016. "Why are we OK with disability drag in Hollywood?" *Los Angeles Times*, July 11. http://www.latimes.com/opinion/op-ed/la-oe-woodburn-ruderman-disability-stats-tv-20160711-snap-story.html.

Wong, Chi-yan and Catherine Tang. 2001. "Understanding heterosexual Chinese college students' intention to adopt safer sex behaviors. *The Journal of Sex Research*, 38 (2): 118–126.

World Health Report. 2017. "World report on disability." Accessed April 12. http://www.who.int/disabilities/world_report/2011/en/.

Worrell, Tracy. 2012. "Why do the voices in my head always say "kill?": An analysis of disability on primetime television." A paper presented at the annual meeting of the National Communication Association, Orlando, FL.

Worrell, Tracy and Heather Zoller. 2004. "President Bartlett has MS: What does that mean for the US?" A paper presented at the annual meeting of the National Communication Association, Chicago, IL.

Ytre-Arne, Brita. 2016. "The Social Media Experiences of Long-Term Patients: Illness, Identity, and Participation." *Nordicom Review*, 37 (1), 57–70.

Zajonc, Robert. 1968. "Attitudinal Effects of Mere Exposure." *Journal of Personality and Social Psychology*, 9, (2): 1–27, doi:10.1037/h0025848.ISSN1939–1315.

———. 2001. "Mere exposure: A gateway to the subliminal." *Current Directions in Psychological Science*, 10 (6): 224–228.

Zhang, Lingling and Beth Haller. 2013. "Consuming Image: How Mass Media Impact the Identity of People with Disabilities." *Communication Quarterly*, 61 (3): 319–334.

Zhou, Shuo, Michael Shapiro, Brian Wansink. 2017. "The Audience Eats More if a Movie Character Keeps Eating: An Unconscious Mechanism for Media Influence on Eating Behaviors." *Appetite*, 108, 407–415. DOI: 10.1016/j.appet.2016.10.028.

Zoller, Heather, and Tracy Worrell. 2006. "Television Illness Depictions, Identity, and Social Experience: Responses to Multiple Sclerosis on *The West Wing* among People with MS." *Health Communication* 20 (1): 69–79. doi:10.1207/s15327027hc2001_7.

Index

Monk, Adrian, 12, 14, 71
multiple personalities, 12
Multiple sclerosis, xi, 36, 83

National Association for Down Syndrome, 6
National Center on Disability and Journalism. *See Disability Language Style Guide*
National Organization on Disability, 9
non-recognition, x

otherness, 53, 63, 100

Paralympic games, xi
Parenthood, 14, 22, 98
parasocial, 22, 79, 84
Parkinson's disease, 3, 22
Pathological model, 63
Patient Protection and Affordable Care Act, 14
perception of self, 36, 37, 57, 60, 73, 82
Performers with Disabilities Tri-Union Committee, 99
portrayals: impact of, xiv, 64, 107; limited, 39, 106; media portrayal, xi, xiv, 13, 31, 50, 52, 57, 69, 72, 73, 74, 77, 78, 82, 95, 99, 100; negative portrayal, x, xi, xiii, 3, 6, 36, 54, 56, 90, 105; of disability, xiii, xiv, 3, 5, 7, 8, 11, 13, 37, 46, 51, 52, 74, 76, 85, 86, 90, 91, 98, 103; physical portrayal, xii, 9; positive portrayal, xi, xiii, xiv, 5, 36, 52, 54, 55, 56, 57, 60, 68, 75, 76, 77, 88, 89, 90, 92, 97, 99
psychotic, 9, 13, 38, 72, 74
public perceptions of illness, xi, 6

regulation, x, 101, 102
regulatory. *See* Regulation
Rehabilitation Act of 1973, 3, 9
reinforcement, xiii, 29, 30, 31, 32, 33, 77
representation, x, xi, xiii, 3, 4, 6, 7, 9, 10, 11, 13, 14, 15, 18, 19, 20, 21, 22, 24, 26, 29, 30, 31, 33, 35, 36, 38, 45, 47, 49, 52, 53, 54, 55, 56, 57, 63, 64, 65, 66, 67, 68, 69, 73, 74, 76, 78, 79, 80, 81, 88, 90, 92, 95, 97, 99, 100, 102, 103, 104, 105, 106, 107; fictional, 4, 21,

37, 60, 103, 104; lack of, 24, 34, 51, 91; misrepresentation, 107; negative, x, 35, 63, 91, 95, 102, 107; positive, x, 39, 55, 57, 66, 76, 101; stereotypical, xi; underrepresentation, 21, 34, 53, 106, 107
respect, x, 33, 73, 90, 91, 100
ridicule, x, 73, 76, 83, 102, 107
Rocky Mountain Americans with Disabilities association, 25
Ross, Karen, 6, 56
Ruderman Studio-Wide Roundtable on Disability Inclusion, 21

Schizophrenia, ix, 4, 7, 10, 12, 80
Screen Actors Guild, 24, 99
The Secret Life of an American Teenager, 3, 12
sense of self, xi, 29, 36, 37, 39, 43, 45, 62, 82, 83
Sesame Street, 10, 55
sign language, 59, 61, 62, 63
Signorelli, Nancy, x, 4, 5, 6, 10, 11, 34, 75
social anxiety. *See* Anxiety
Social cognitive theory, xiv, 29, 30, 31, 32, 38, 50, 51, 77, 91
Social construction, xi, xiii, xiv, 4, 38, 45, 62, 71, 72, 73, 74, 77, 79
Social identity theory. *See* identity, social
social learning. *See* Social cognitive theory
social media, xiii, 1, 22, 34, 39, 41, 43, 44, 45, 46, 79, 83, 100, 105
social model of disability, 4
social norms, xiv, 32
Social Security, 6; Act in 1935, 6
social support, xii, 43, 62
societal attitude. *See* Attitudes
societal influences, 4
Society of Professional Journalists, 100
Speechless, 14, 17, 106
stereotype, xi, 5, 6, 11, 13, 15, 17, 19, 21, 34, 39, 45, 52, 54, 56, 69, 72, 75, 76, 77, 79, 81, 91, 98, 99, 102, 103, 104, 105; fool, 5, 6, 19, 23; hero, 5, 6, 19, 99; victim, ix, x, 5, 7, 11, 13, 18, 22, 25, 54, 60, 78, 91; villain, 5, 6, 13, 53
stereotypical representation. *See* Representation

About the Author

Dr. Tracy Worrell is an associate professor in the School of Communication at the Rochester Institute of Technology. Dr. Worrell's primary research area is in examining health messages and the media, specifically looking at disability. She has written numerous national and international conference papers and has been published in journals such as *Health Communication*. Publications have explored areas such as the portrayal of illness on television and its impact on those with said illnesses to creating effective health messages to promote behavior change. Dr. Worrell received her PhD in Communication from Michigan State University her MA from the University of Cincinnati and BA from Otterbein University.